St Andrews

& THE OPEN CHAMPIONSHIP

THE OFFICIAL HISTORY

BY DAVID JOY WITH PHOTOGRAPHY BY IAIN MACFARLANE LOWE

Sleeping Bear Press

Sleeping Bear Press
121 South Main
P.O. Box 20
Chelsea, Michigan 48118
www.sleepingbearpress.com

Printed and bound in Canada by Friesens, Altona, Manitoba.
10 9 8 7 6 5 4 3 2 1

Joy, David.
St Andrews & the open championship: the official history / by David Joy with photographs by Iain Macfarlane Lowe.
p. cm.
ISBN 1-886947-26-0
1. St Andrews Open (Golf tournament) --History. 2. Royal and Ancient Golf Club of St Andrews--History.
I. Title. II. Title: St Andrews Open championships.
GV970.3.S72J69   1999
796.352 ' 66--dc21 99-33454
CIP

Inquiries for reproduction of the course imagery or photography should be directed to: www.st-andrews-studio.co.uk
or write to: Iain Lowe, St Andrews Studio, 10 Fergusson Place, St Andrews, Fife KY16 9NF, UK.

To my father, D.L. Joy, an active member of the St Andrews Golf Club for 62 years—and still swinging.
—*David Joy*

To my wife, Muriel, and son, Chris, for their continual support and encouragement.
—*Iain Macfarlane Lowe*

Iain and I must mention that the book would not have been possible without the help of The George Cowie Collection—University of St Andrews, D.C. Thomsons of Dundee, The St Andrews Preservation Trust, The Prestwick Golf Club, *Golf Weekly* (for the *Golf Illustrated* insertions), and the St Andrews Links Trust for their support.

As the Swilken Burn meanders across the course, I wonder just how much water has flowed through it since the Society of St Andrews Golfers crossed it during their first club medal in 1754.

The Birth

of a

Championship

Introduction

PEOPLE WHO HAVE PAID HOMAGE TO ST ANDREWS, AND IN PARTICULAR TO THE OPEN

CHAMPIONSHIPS HOSTED IN "THE HOME OF GOLF," ARE SURPRISED WHEN THEY LOOK

AROUND AT THE LAYERS OF ANTIQUITY NOW DORMANT IN THE TOWN.

Behind the familiar image of the Royal and Ancient Clubhouse stands the old gray city with its square tower, spires, and twin towers. "Just aim on the steeple, sir" is the caddie's timeless cry from the links.

"Muckross"—a Pictish word for "headland of swine" or "land of the wild boar"—was the original name of St Andrews some 6,000 years ago.

St Regulus was reputedly shipwrecked off this coastline in the fourth century with 16 monks, two devoted virgins, and a cask containing the knee bone and two index fingers of St Andrew!

It has always been a pilgrim city throughout its long and turbulent history. It was a walled city, for which you needed a pass to enter. It was the ecclesiastical capital of Scotland, with a magnificent cathedral founded in the early twelfth century, when the common ground, later known as the "Linksland," was bequeathed to the town's residents. It was their right to use it as they saw fit—for recreation (maybe even golf!), or for breeding rabbits. The city grew with the building of the cathedral, which was eventually consecrated by Robert the Bruce in 1318.

A formidable castle on the cliff looking out over the North Sea schooled the young King Jameses of the fifteenth century. At that time notices were placed banning golf on the Sabbath for interfering with archery practice—which was compulsory for the defence of the Realm.

The University of St Andrews, the oldest in Scotland, was founded in 1412. One of the early references to golf in St Andrews was from the diary of student James Melville, in 1574. He wrote that his father had provided him with

"glub an' bals fur goff but nocht a purss fur catch pull and tavern." Translated, this reads: "club and balls for golf but nothing for hand tennis or drinking in the pub."

Just 20 years earlier Archbishop Hamilton had acknowledged a licence granting him permission "to plant cuniggis in the links" (to breed rabbits) as long as it did not interfere with the rights of the locals to play "golff"—or gouff, goff, gowf, gow'lf, or kolf! Spelling was obviously not part of the educational curriculum of that time!

The Reformation did not just tear the heart out of St Andrews—it decimated it. In 1559, incited by John Knox, who had ranted for nearly three days from the pulpit in the town church, a mob ransacked and burnt down the cathedral. Prior to this, seven martyrs had been burnt at the stake at different points in the centre of the town—and for what? Freedom of speech? The town did not recover from such trauma and was nearly bankrupt until golf was popularised some 300 years later.

During those dark years the university kept its profile as a great seat of learning. Benjamin Franklin studied and graduated from the University. Later, in 1759, it awarded him an honorary degree. In that same year he was made an Honorary Burgess and granted The Freedom of the City. Two hundred years later another American, Bobby Jones, was given that same honour.

The dollar sign ($) was "invented" at the University by a Fife man, John Bain.

Three of the 12 signatories on the American Declaration of Independence were St Andrews graduates!

A winter scene from the eighth tee with the skyline of "The Auld Gray Toon."

But enough of sound bites and exclamation marks! On to the Links itself, or "The Metropolis of Golfing" as it was referred to in the seventeenth and eighteenth centuries—even though there was hardly anyone playing! The Society of St Andrews Golfers, founded in 1754, gave credence to this "Metropolis," and the game became more established. In 1834 royal patronage was given by King William, and the Society from that moment on was to be called The Royal and Ancient Golf Club.

The R&A's membership was mainly restricted to noblemen and gentlemen, who mainly played in spring and autumn meetings, as they still do today. Red jackets with yellow buttons were the first "uniforms" they wore. Earl St Clair of Roslin, with 121 strokes, is the only recorded score found on the 22-hole course in 1764, for the next day the members decided that the first four holes were too short and converted them into two.

This needs explaining. The original course was 11 holes. You played the 11 out to the estuary, then round and played them all back again—outward players simply "giving way" on the greens to the gentlemen playing in. Having converted to nine holes with the same routine back, 18 holes were played. The course was played in the reverse of how it is today. Having acquired more ground and created the now-famous big double greens, this eased the congestion. With more and more gentlemen playing, the course was played clockwise one week—and anticlockwise (as it is always played now) the next. This gave the course the respite it needed from "excessive wear and tear," with hardly any maintenance involved.

To the right of the last fairway, on the site that is now Rusacks Hotel, was the communal drying green and lifeboat shed. The road now splitting the first and eighteenth across the middle was originally a well-worn track for pulling the lifeboat to the sea. Up by the last green is Allan Robertson's cottage, where feather balls were made and handed out. Beside him Hugh Philp laboured in his workshop, where he made much sought after, hand-crafted, goosenecked clubs—valued collector's items today. Behind is The Old Union Parlour, which was used as a clubhouse before the R&A was built. Next door to it is a building now used by David Hill, Championship Secretary, and his team for the administration of the British Open.

The town and the Links were run-down until Lieutenant Colonel Sir Hugh Lyon Playfair, in the 1840s, took it by the scruff of the neck and knocked it back into shape. Chief Magistrate and Provost, he instigated "Forty Rules and Regulations—which must be obeyed," for example, "All slaughter-houses' and fish curers' premises shall be cleaned and the dung and offal removed daily during the months from June to September—and no person shall be allowed to accumulate more than one ton on his premises."

Playfair had been instrumental in setting up The Old Union Parlour and in founding the Royal and Ancient Clubhouse. He had the town hall built and organised the construction of a railway track joining the main line some three miles out of the city. He even bought the train!

The impact of the new lease of life he had given to the town was immense. He started promoting tourism, so effectively that *The Fifeshire Journal* described the Links in the summer of 1850 as, "every evening populated by hundreds of all sexes, sizes and grades, to witness or participate in what is going forward. Bowls, tossing the caber, putting the stone or iron ball, quoits, skittles, hammer-throwing, football, even cricket, were all going on at once, and tending to get mixed up with the golfers, and putting them off their aim. Add that ladies would take an airing in their carriages across the Links and older golfers would even ride ponies between strokes on the fairway."

POLICE BYE-LAWS & REGULATIONS
MADE BY THE
PROVOST, MAGISTRATES, AND TOWN COUNCIL
OF ST ANDREWS.

The Provost, Magistrates, and Town Council of St Andrews, by virtue of the powers conferred on them by the Acts 3 and 4, William IV., Cap. 46, and 10 and 11, Victoria, Cap. 39, do hereby enact and regulate as follows, viz :—

1. No Ashes, Filth, or refuse of any kind shall at any time be thrown from doors, windows, or stairs, upon the Streets or Lanes, but shall be kept in backets, and taken to the Scavengers' Carts or Barrows, which will pass every lawful day and twice on Saturdays.—Liquids may be poured into the gutters, but carefully, so as not to spread over the Streets, and shall on no account be thrown from doors, stairs, or windows.

2. All Slaughter-Houses and Fish Curers Premises shall be cleaned and the Dung and offal removed daily during the months from June to September inclusive, and shall be cleaned and removed once every three days during the rest of the year.—All other receptacles for Dung shall be cleaned out once a week during said period from June to September inclusive, and once a fortnight during the rest of the year;—and no person shall be allowed to accumulate more than one ton on his premises.—No Dung shall remain on the Streets more than one hour previous to removal; and from the 1st day of March to the 1st day of November, the whole shall be removed before 9 o'clock A.M., and during the rest of the year, before 10 o'clock A.M.—Failing removal within the

Far left: A large hand-painted map of the Old Course, which hangs in the R&A. It illustrates all of the feature bunkers on the course and includes a map of the town.

Left: "Forty rules and regulations that must be obeyed!" 1843.

This aerial shot shows how the course is very much an integral part of St Andrews. The three main streets of Market Street, North Street, and South Street have been in existence since the twelfth century.

Out on the course, circa 1856.

The eleventh was such an intransigent green that Old Tom Morris used to dread going out to inspect it—fearful that it might not even be there! With shifting sand, the hole, more often than not, collapsed in on itself or became as big as the Balmoral bonnet that the gentlemen is wearing in the illustration, on a busy Medal day. It was because of the problem with this green that, in 1865, Tom Morris had the idea of using the first metal cup to keep the hole in place.

Articles & Laws in playing the Golf

1 You must Tee your Ball within a Club length of the Hole

2 Your Tee must be upon the Ground

3 You are not to change the Ball which you Strike off the Tee.

4 You are not to remove Stones, Bones or any Break Club for the Sake of playing your Ball, Except upon the fair Green, and that only within a Club length of your Ball.

5 If your Ball come among Water, or any Watery filth, You are at Liberty to take out your Ball, and throwing it behind the hazard six yards at least, You may play it with any Club, and allow your Adversary a Stroke, for so getting out your Ball.

6 If your Balls be found any where touching one another, You are to lift the first Ball, till you play the last.

7 At Holeing, You are to play your Ball honestly for the Hole, and not to play upon your Adversary's Ball, not lying in your way to the Hole

8 If you should lose your Ball, by its being taken up, or any other way You are to go back to the Spot, where you Struck last, and drop another Ball, and allow your Adversary a Stroke for the Misfortune

9 No Man at Holeing his Ball, is to be allowed to Mark his way to the Hole with his Club or any thing else.

10 If a Ball be Stop'd by any person, Horse, Dog, or any thing else, the Ball so Stop'd must be played where it lyes.

11 If you draw your Club in order to Strike, and proceed so far in the Stroke as to be bringing down your Club; if then your Club shall break, in any way, it is to be Accounted a Stroke.

12 He, whose Ball lyes furthest from the Hole is obliged to play first

13 Neither Trench, Ditch, or Dyke made for the preservation of the Links, Nor the Scholars holes or the Soldiers Lines Shall be Accounted a Hazard, But the Ball is to be taken out Teed and played with any Iron Club.

Articles of Law—The Thirteen Rules of Golf—adopted by the Society of St Andrews Golfers when founded in 1754.

The St Andrews Bay created a sheltered area where galleons could sail in and out of the harbor on short freighting runs, but as trains took over the trade died. The livelihood of the fisherfolk was threatened and most of the men were grateful for the opportunity to supplement their income by caddying.

"Just aim on the steeple, sir" was the spire of St Salvator's, one of the oldest and most prominent parts of the fifteenth century university. Where this photograph was taken shows the fishermen's quarters toward the ruin of the cathedral. The Ladyhead, as it was called, bred five Open champions. As boys, the street was their fairway, and gas lamps their flags, as they whacked wine corks or whatever would substitute as a ball with their first sawn-down club in their hands.

The tollbooth in the center of the cobbled end of Market Street was also used as the town jail until 1856. The gentlemen golfers were piped down to the course from here for the start of their Spring and Autumn Meetings. To the right is Stewart's Hotel (later to become the Cross Keys) the venue for the first Grand Balls of the Royal and Ancient Golf Club.

Lieutenant Colonel Sir Hugh Lyon Playfair, Chief Magistrate and Provost in the 1840s who, almost single-handedly "cleaned up the town!"

The Union Parlour was established before the Royal and Ancient Clubhouse was built in 1854. It was located behind the last green as a meeting place and facility for the few gentlemen who played the game on a regular basis.

Below: This is the first photograph taken of the Home Hole in the late 1840s with golf in progress.

Students of St Andrews University at play, in and around "Cheape's" bunker on the second hole in 1855.

This map of the Old Course drawn up in 1821 shows the original nine holes set in 1764 and played in the reverse of how it is today. You simply gave way on the greens to the incoming matches, who, after reaching the estuary, turned around, and played the same holes back again.

Posed photograph down the fairway of the Home Hole in the 1850s. The railway station was situated by the edge of the second green (now the sixteenth) but had to be moved into town when the merchants of Edinburgh and Perth got off the trains and straight on to the course. What looks like snow down the second fairway is, in fact, linen laid out on whins to bleach in the sun.

As the canon blasts at precisely 8:00am, the new Captain of the Royal and Ancient plays himself into office on the last day of the Autumn Meeting. The caddies are lined up down the fairway ready for his drive, and whoever retrieves the ball and returns it, receives a gold sovereign in exchange.

A familiar view of the first and eighteenth with cars crossing the middle of the fairway. The road was originally used as a track for pulling a lifeboat across from the communal drying green beside Granny Clark's Wynd!

Above and opposite page: Two contrasting moods—at dawn and dusk on the fourteenth, with the heather in bloom.

The Prelude

TOM MORRIS IS THE FIGUREHEAD IN SHOWING HOW DRAMATICALLY THE GAME EVOLVED DURING HIS LONG LIFETIME (1821-1908). HE IS REFERRED TO IN SOME SHAPE OR FORM IN EVERY OPEN REPORT UP UNTIL HIS RETIREMENT AS KEEPER OF THE GREEN OR CUSTODIAN OF THE LINKS OF ST ANDREWS IN 1902. A BORN AND BRED ST ANDREAN, HE OFTEN USED TO SAY "WE WERE AW BORN WI' WEBBED FEET AND A GOLF CLUB IN OUR HAND HERE."

Morris started his legendary career as a feather ball maker apprenticed to Allan Robertson, who was given the dubious title of "The World's First Golf Professional." Robertson was the only player who actually practised his game and played against the course rather than in matches. Robertson was unbeatable in his day (though he chose his matches carefully). It was considered miraculous when he broke 80 on the Old Course on the 15th of September 1858 while playing with Mr Bethune of Blebo. With the equipment used and the severity of the Old Course at that time, the average score in winning a medal was about 105. Robertson's feat was achieved playing with a hand-hammered "gutty."

The emergence of the gutta-percha ball in 1848 was the biggest factor in what was to be a dramatic surge in the number of people playing the game—that, and the railway lines connecting up our Linkslands (Linksland being the link between the sea and the arable ground). The ball and the train had made golf and the course accessible—although it would take another 30 years to popularise the playing of the game.

The first "Grand Tournament" was played a couple of years after the Royal and Ancient Clubhouse was built in 1854. The 12 established clubs in existence at that time were each invited to send two "gentlemen golfers" (amateurs) to compete.

The players (professionals)—who had been caddying for the gentlemen in the morning—were paired to play against each other in the tournament in the afternoon. It was the Dunn brothers or the Parks versus Robertson and Morris, who were never beaten in foursomes up until the untimely death of Allan Robertson one year before the first Open.

With Tom Morris losing his livelihood as a ball maker in St Andrews, he had been invited to Prestwick in 1851 to "mark out a green" that, as a 12-hole course, was to host the first Open in 1860. "Please send a respectable caddie," was the invitation sent to six clubs.

Eight players competed, and Willie Park from Musselburgh beat Tom Morris by two shots.

Morris was not too disappointed, for he won £3 as the runner-up. Park, as the winner, received no prize money, but had the honour of being known as The Champion Golfer of the year.

All of the early Opens were played at Prestwick over three

Steps take you down into "Sahara" bunker in front of the seventeenth green with the links and town of Prestwick behind.

rounds on the day. Tom Morris won four, his last in 1867, at age 46. He was the oldest winner, followed the next year by the youngest—his son Tommy, just 17 years old. Son and father were winner and runner-up in the 1869 Open when the younger Morris, with a record 49 in the last round of the 12-hole course, beat his father by three shots.

In 1861, the main sponsor and presenter of The Challenge Belt, the Earl of Eglington, died, followed by the sole administrator of the event, J.O. Fairlie, in 1870. This was the same year that Young Tom Morris won the Championship for a third time in succession (by 12 shots) and therefore got to keep The Challenge Belt.

The Belt

The Challenge Belt was similar to a jousting or archery trophy, which Eglington and Fairlie would have competed against each other for earlier that century! The Belt was of a soft Moroccan leather. The main buckle was hand-engraved with a detailed golfing scene. It is unfortunate

that the earl did not live long enough to present another belt. I am sure he would not have allowed another belt to become the possession of another three-time winner. It could still have been played for today, thus adding a touch more theatre and a greater sense of history to the championship.

The Prestwick Club decided to invite St Andrews and Musselburgh to host the Open, thus easing the burden of continuously organising the event and immediately having to provide a new trophy. There was no championship or challenge in 1871 because Prestwick had yet to reach an agreement with the other two bodies as to how the tournament would progress. They had not deemed it important enough to call a special meeting.

A claret jug had been subscribed for and purchased for the 1872 Open. This would seem a most appropriate trophy, as most of the gentlemen's wagers in matchplay in bygone days were for bottles—or indeed cases!—of claret. Tom Morris Jr—seemingly invincible—won yet again.

The Challenge Belt was presented by the Earl of Eglington for the championship at Prestwick in 1860.

Willie Park from Musselburgh was the first Open Champion in 1860 and winner again in 1863, '66, and '75. All his wins were at Prestwick, where he was also runner-up on four occasions.

Knights in shining armour—The Earl of Eglington (above) and James Ogilvie Fairlie (right), past Captains of the Royal and Ancient Golf Club— the sponsor and the Championship Secretary of the first Open!

A studio portrait of Tom Morris in his prime in the mid-1850s. Note the open stance and the "hammer" grip.

This is part of a letter from J.O. Fairlie to George Glennie in Blackheath (near London) inviting him to send "a respectable caddie" to play in the first Open. Eight competitors entered the fray and were— William Park of Musselburgh; Tom Morris, Prestwick; Steele and Smith, Bruntsfield; George Brown, Blackheath; Andrew Strath, St Andrews; Charlie Hunter of the St Nicholas Club, Prestwick; and Andrew "The Rock," Perth.

After the First World War the R&A accepted full responsibility for running the championship wherever it was to be played. As the media, "the hype," and all the lucrative commercial aspects of the game grew—so too did the organisation and administration of it. From the right ship run by Brigadier Brickman, Keith McKenzie emerged and was to be known as "Mr Open" for the way he kept up with the rapid advance of the championship in a more commercial but discretionary manner. He had huge respect within the golfing community for his integrity and his accessibility.

McKenzie was followed by Michael Bonallack, equally respected, who as a golfer had an impressive record of wins in the Amateur championship to his name. He also played in the Open championship itself and made the cut on three occasions. He recently received a Knighthood in recognition of his services to the game and retired prior to the millennium Open. Sir Michael was immediately elected Captain of the Royal and Ancient Golf Club for that year instead! The new Secretary, Peter Dawson, has a hard

Keith McKenzie

Sir Michael Bonallack

act to follow, but will be backed up by David Hill, the Championship Secretary, who although still a relatively young man, already has 20 years of experience in its running.

The main competitors in a tournament at Leith in 1867. Includes three past winners—Andrew Strath (bottom of steps, left), Tom Morris Senior and Junior (top and bottom of steps, right), and Jamie Anderson, a future three-time winner (far right).

Tom Morris in 1861 after his first of four Open Championship wins.

Allan Robertson and Tom Morris (second and third left), watch Mr Campbell attempt to putt out on the Old Course in the Spring Meeting of 1850. Next to him is Sandy Pirie, Keeper of the Green, carrying the clubs. Sir Thomas Moncriefie and Colonel Fairlie look on.

Young Tom's winning scorecard in the 1870 Open. Two rounds recorded on the front and one on the back of the same card. In defending his title for the third year in succession he opened up with a record 47, which was never beaten on the original 12-hole course at Prestwick. Its conversion to 18 holes took place prior to hosting the 1884 championship. On winning The Championship Belt three years in succession, it was Young Tom's to keep. He won that year by 12 shots. In 1862 his father, Tom Morris Sr, had won with the biggest margin ever recorded in the history of the Open—by 13 shots. The fact that there were only four professionals playing that day was a minor detail from Old Tom's point of view!

Medal with an inscription added to The Challenge Belt in 1868.

The Claret Jug replaced The Challenge Belt in 1872 and it is still played for today.

The Morrises, father and son, oldest and youngest ever winners of the Open, both won four times during the first 12 years of the Championship.
Tom Morris Sr - 1861, '62, '64, '67.
Tom Morris Jr - 1868, '69, '70, '72.

The Grand National Tournament 1857

Two gentlemen golfers (amateurs) represented each of the 12 established clubs in existence at that time. They came from Edinburgh, Leith, Perth, North Berwick, Montrose, Monifieth, Aberdeen, Prestwick, and Blackheath, representing England. Blackheath won, in fact, but this was considered acceptable by the Scottish teams as Mr Glennie and Mr Stewart, representing the club, were both Scots.

"Allan Robertson the greatest golf player that ever lived, of whom alone in the annals of the pastime it can be said that he was never beaten," read his obituary, just one year before the start of the Open. He was 42 years old.

Right: Illustration by the author of the original "Big Three,"—Park, Morris, and Robertson.

Right: A foursomes match. Robertson (swinging) and Morris versus Park and Dunn—St Andrews versus Musselburgh. After caddying for their gentlemen in the morning round of the Grand Tournament, the professionals would be matched against each other in the afternoon, with many a wager struck between the members out on the course following the game.

Thomas Rodger was the first to have a photographic studio in the town and set up this shot of Mr Thomas Chambers (on a long exposure) holing out on the last green, after winning "The Grand Tournament of 1856."

The inscription on the belt clasp..."Tom Morris Jr— Championship Golfer."

"The Grand Old Man of Golf." Tom Morris's appearance altered dramatically from the 1850s into the next two decades until the more familiar image evolved of the old man with the white beard, out walking the Old Course.

Major Boothby lines up a shot on the first green (now the seventeenth)—watched by Tom Morris and Allan Robertson on the Swilken Bridge.

1873

AND SO IT WAS THAT, IN EARLY OCTOBER 1873, "THE CHALLENGE TROPHY" WAS PLAYED ON THE OLD COURSE AT ST ANDREWS FOR THE FIRST TIME.

The future of the Open seemed secure. An announcement went out in *The Field* magazine saying that a cup had been procured for annual competition to be open to all comers. Unlike The Challenge Belt, "this trophy can never become the absolute property of any winner, but along with the custody of it for one year, he gets a medal to be specially retained and also a money prize (£11). It will be observed that the Championship competition is now thoroughly established which will tend to increase the popularity of this elegant and healthy pastime."

Mr D. McWhannel, a gentleman representing the Royal and Ancient Golf Club, had the honour of being the first man to tee off in a St Andrews Open, along with his friend and partner Mr Henry Lamb. The Old Course would host two 18-hole rounds that day to determine the outcome. Tom Morris Jr was the odds-on favourite, and of course his father was expected to be in contention—despite being 52 years old. Old Tom's great sparring partner, Willie Park, did not travel from Musselburgh. It was in fact worrisome that so few had made the effort to come through. To quote from the *St Andrews Citizen*, "The list of competitors is chiefly remarkable for the absence of the names of professional players from a distance, the majority of the competitors being amateurs." Of the 13 pairings, the only

players not from St Andrews were Bob Pringle, representing Musselburgh, and William Thomson, representing Edinburgh. Jack Morris (Young Tom's cousin) had taken up the post of professional at Hoylake and travelled up to enter the fray, but he failed to record a score.

It seems strange that on an idyllic golfing day the scoring should be so high, but then it appeared that the course was waterlogged after days of rain. A one-shot penalty would have been enforced at that time for a "pick and drop," so Young Tom and the main contenders, it would seem, must have had very wet socks by the end of the day. The aggregate of 179 by the winner, Tom Kidd, was to be the highest ever recorded.

Puddles, heavy rain, and even flash floods have been major factors in the outcome at St Andrews through 25 championships. I wonder how deflated Tom Kidd was, when reading one of the main reports the next week in *The Fifeshire Journal*, he saw, "It was scarcely anticipated that Kidd would carry off the palm. As a player he is likely to improve."

Tom Kidd was popular on the links, spending most of his summer months from then on as a registered caddie and player. It was a shock to the town when he died suddenly in 1884, aged 35.

Unseen from the fourteenth tee, "the Beardies," a group of three bunkers, wait to catch a drive hit slightly left.

Tom Kidd, the unexpected winner of the first Open at St Andrews.

The view of the Old Course and the Royal and Ancient Clubhouse from the West Sands, just prior to the first Open Championship played there in 1873.

The First 'Open' at St. Andrews

The annual competition for the Champion Golf Trophy (a Silver Challenge Cup and Gold Medal to remain the property of the winner) and money prizes to the value of £25, came off at St. Andrews on Saturday. The weather, after several days' constant rain, cleared beautifully up, and proved very favourable for the competition. The Links were much saturated with water and proved heavy to play over in consequence. The match consisted in two rounds of the Links or 36 holes, and was decided by strokes, not holes. The spectators on the green were very numerous, and seemed deeply interested in the result. Thirteen couples competed.

At the close of the second round the result was found to be as follows:—

Tom Kidd, 179—Champion and 1st prize.
Jamie Anderson, 180—2nd prize.
Tom Morris, jun.⎫183—3rd and
Bob Kirk   ⎭   4th prizes
David Strath, 187—5th prize.

The next best were: Tom Morris, sen., 189; Mr H. A. Lamb, 192; Robert Martin and William Fernie, 194; Mr Robert Armit, J. O. F. Morris, and James Fenton, 195; Mr Mure Fergusson, 199; and T. Mansie, 200.

Tom Kidd, who has by the result of this competition won for himself the high honour of champion, has already proved himself to be an excellent player, and distinguished himself in many singles and foursomes, and the honour thus gained will consequently be grudged him the less, although he has won it with so high a score.

The first report in *The Fifeshire Journal.*

Young Tom, wearing his Balmoral bonnet. So much power and effort went into his long shots that his bonnet was frequently falling off his head!

Tom Kidd in 1873.

The youngest of the Morrises, J.O.F., lines up a putt.

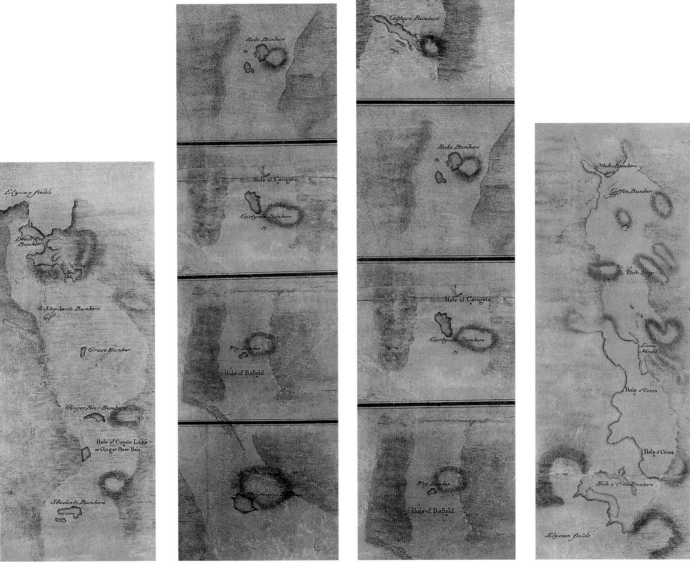

"I may here mention that the Royal Golf Club has a lithographed plan of the course in which all the bunkers, as well as other features on the ground, are laid down by name with all the care exercised in indicating sand-banks and sunk rocks in a mariners chart. An exact knowledge of topography of the Links may well be supposed to be of the greatest consequence, where the ground is so various and in general so difficult."—*Chambers Journal*-October, 1842

1876

THE "AULD GREY TOON" WAS NOW LIVING UP TO ITS NAME, WITH AN AIR OF GLOOMY DESPONDENCY HANGING AROUND IT SINCE THE END OF 1875 AND THE SAD DEMISE OF ITS LOCAL HERO, TOM MORRIS JR. IT IS AN IMPORTANT STORY TO BE TOLD HERE BECAUSE IF NOT FOR HIS UNTIMELY DEATH HE WOULD SURELY HAVE DOMINATED THE CHAMPIONSHIP AND ITS HISTORY FOR MANY YEARS.

6th September 1875—on that day, the Morrises played a match against the Park brothers at North Berwick. Tommy wasn't keen to travel, for his wife Margaret was heavy with child. They had been married for just under a year. She was a striking red-haired woman, and what a bonny couple they made.

Anyway, Old Tom was keen to play and Margaret encouraged them to play, as it was a £25-a-side challenge. They went, and, in front of a big crowd, were winning easily until they hit a bit of sand on the back few holes. The Parks—Willie and Mungo—came back at them. The Morrises just managed to hang in, and won on the last green.

They came off the course to a mixed reception, for the Parks had brought a large support with them from Musselburgh and Edinburgh. A telegram had arrived saying that Tommy should make his way "post haste" to St Andrews, as his wife was struggling with the child.

It would be a long, tedious journey back by train, changing at Edinburgh and Granton, then by steamer to Burntisland, then another train to Ladybank, changing again for Leuchars and again for St Andrews. A Mr Lewis, one of the sponsors of the game, offered his schooner and full crew to take them straight across the Firth of Forth and home—which they gratefully accepted. As they were leaving,

unbeknown to them, another telegram had arrived saying that both Margaret and the child, a boy, had died.

Later in life—when he could finally bring himself to talk about it—Tom Morris Sr said, "It was a long, weary crossing. That frozen look Tommy had on his face haunts me still, like the early photographs I still carry of him. My brother George met us in a wee rowing boat out in the bay and told me the news. I had to tell him straight away. He cried out, "It's no' true!" Aye, but it was. I sat out in that bay for over two hours trying to calm the boy, and then rowed him into the harbour. It was a sad, pathetic homecoming."

Tommy's grief was insurmountable. His family and his friends all tried to pull him out of his misery. He started drinking, though previously he had hardly taken a drink in his life apart from Christmas and New Year's Eve. His drinking got steadily worse, and his heart just wasn't in anything. It was up in the cathedral grounds with his wife and bairn.

After much persuasion, a golf match was set up with the Morrises against Davie Strath and Bob Martin, great adversaries of theirs, and the whole town came out to see it. Tommy showed some signs of his old self, but on the fourteenth tee, four up, he just broke down and they lost the last five holes and the match.

Tommy became even more disconsolate as Old Tom had one last try to get him back into his golf. A Captain Molesworth had put out an advert in the *Scottish Field* that his son would challenge any professional to a third (meaning that he would get a shot every third hole). Tommy was not keen, but after a lot of bullying and cajoling, he reluctantly agreed.

Beginning of November it was, with biting winds and frost on a hostile Old Course. They played 12 rounds in six days. Tommy was winning easily, but because he was so run-down, he was chilled to the marrow. Molesworth insisted they play on.

Tommy developed pneumonia after that and went downhill very quickly. At one point it seemed he might rally. Just one week before Christmas, he went to visit some friends in Edinburgh. He came back on Christmas Eve and went upstairs to visit his mother—she was an invalid by this time—then went to his bed.

Old Tom said, "I heard him get up on Christmas morning—when he wasn't coming down I went up to see, and there he was lying as peaceful as I'd seen him since Margaret had died.

He was dead. Because of the suddenness of it, they did an autopsy at the cottage hospital. They said he had burst an artery in his lung. People say he died of a broken heart—but if that could really happen then I wouldn't be here either!"

Elegy of Tom Morris Jr

Beneath the sod poor Tommy's laid
Bunkered now for good and all
A finer golfer never played
A further or a surer ball

Among the monarchs of the green
For long he held imperial sway
And none the start and end between
Could match with Tommy on his day

A triple laurel round his brow
The light of triumph in his e'e
He stands before us even now
As in his hour of victory

Thrice belted knight of peerless skill
Again we see him head the fray
And memory loves to reckon still
The feats of Tommy on his day

On Tuesday 25th September, 1876, Prince Leopold (the fifth son of Queen Victoria) arrived to be installed as Captain of the Royal and Ancient at the start of the Autumn Meeting. It was to be the most colourful three days of the buildup to the Open in its history. It caused great excitement in the town. Fluttering handkerchiefs and lusty cheers greeted the prince as his carriage and entourage rode into the main street. Lined with hundreds of folk, the streets were bedecked with streamers, bunting, flags and banners. The Town Council and local dignitaries were all grouped outside the Royal Hotel—appropriately enough—to acknowledge the first royal visit since Charles the Second some 200 years earlier.

Late on Wednesday morning the prince played himself in on the first tee. According to the *Fife Herald*, "The ball was teed for his Royal Highness by Tom Morris, and the prince opened by striking off the first ball, and so became holder of the Royal Adelaide Medal and Silver Club. His Royal Highness struck the ball very fairly, sending it over the heads of the spectators. The prince, as is well known to golfers, is by no means a novice in the Royal game."

The next day the prince partnered Tom Morris against John Whyte Melville—a distinguished past captain—and Sir Robert Anstruther in a "short match" (three out and three in), which was followed by a huge crowd. The prince won comfortably, with a little help from Old Tom.

Many of the professional players had come across for the arrival of the prince with the hopes of playing some challenge matches to supplement their incomes prior to the main event. Davie Strath, Young Tom's great friend and sparring partner, was in terrific form and beat Mungo Park (who had won the Championship in 1874) by seven holes. Willie Park, the defending and four-time champion, was looking for games, and local favourites Bob Kirk and Jamie Anderson were intent on sharpening up their game throughout the week.

The town was packed to the gunnels with a ratio of 100 onlookers to every participant involved in the week's proceedings.

It is worth describing the setting for the Ball on Wednesday evening, for it was to mark the climax of a golden era for the lords and ladies of the old fox and hounds brigade.

The Ball

The town hall had been splendidly decorated with the R&A's silver clubs, balls, and medals suspended over a royal canopy of scarlet cloth with the words "Royal and Ancient." This was hung over a semicircle in blue and white calico with the prince's coat of arms centred. At the foot of the hall was placed a large mirror with rare tropical plants to the fore, while over it hung the crest of the retiring captain, the Honourable Charles Carnegie. The whole design represented a pavilion. The walls were hung with scarlet cloth trimmed with mirrors panelled with fluted columns, each window filled with a semicircular fan with royal crests and mottoes. The orchestra wore scarlet and was surrounded by evergreens and flowers.

The ball was led off by Prince Leopold and the Countess of Rothes at 10:00pm, Sir Robert Anstruther dancing with the Countess of Rosslyn in the opposite set. The dancing was kept up, as were their horses and carriages, 'til the early hours of the morning "with the greatest spirit." The printed programme stated the order of dances was, "a waltz, a waltz, galop, waltz, reel, galop, quadrille, waltz, galop, country dance, waltz, galop, quadrille, waltz, galop"…and on and on it went in what was to become that class of society's last great highland fling.

The Illuminations

The next evening saw the town lit up between the hours of 9:00 and 10:00. The residents were asked to turn up their gas lamps and pull open their curtains to shed light on the scarlet drapes, flowers, wreaths, evergreens, and flags hanging from every building. A large bonfire in the centre of the town was lit, and gas jets were directed into the shape of a crown on top of the town church. Hundreds of small coloured lights and Chinese lanterns highlighted the many banners inscribed with "God Save the Queen—Welcome to HRH Prince Leopold—Our Queen and Country."

Telegram to the Queen—Friday 28th September:

"The prince left this morning at ten. The Artillery Company lined the platform. When the train left, a large crowd loudly and enthusiastically cheered the prince. The morning is very wet."

It was an extraordinary affair which nearly bankrupted the local council and gentry involved.

The reason for reporting all this prior to the Open is that it disrupted the busy schedule of all the games normally played by the R&A, which, by the time the Championship was held on Saturday, created chaos, with so many members and guests wanting to play and no block of times booked for the Open competitors.

The Championship (At Last)

On top of all this, it was reported, "The circumstances for play were rather unfavourable; showery—greens heavy."

Davie Strath, the local favourite—but representing North Berwick—eventually got under way. He was paired for both rounds with Bob Dow of Montrose and they were followed by a large crowd. Everyone that played (there were 19 entered) had spectators milling around them. Four retired after the first round, including Mr Tom Maurice of Blackheath, which must have confused the Tom Morris camp! Games backed up against each other and players and greens were unsighted during play, which was to be the ultimate downfall of Strath.

Bob Martin of St Andrews (last year's runner-up at Prestwick) started well, going out in 42, with Strath just one stroke behind.

It is worth recording some of the main contenders' figures just to show how difficult it was to score well, especially on the last six holes.

First Round

Strath
Out	5 5 4 6 6 5 4 4 4 – 43	
In	3 4 4 6 6 6 4 5 5 – 43	**86**

(He stubbed and missed a two-inch putt at the 15th.)

Martin
Out	5 5 5 6 5 4 4 4 4 – 42	
In	5 3 3 6 5 5 5 7 5 – 44	**86**

Tom Morris and Willie Park were watched with great interest. Park was considered to have had bad luck in an opening round of 94.

Morris
Out	6 6 5 5 5 5 5 3 4 – 44	
In	5 3 3 5 7 6 6 6 5 – 46	**90**

Second Round

Martin
Out	5 5 4 5 7 6 5 3 5 – 45	
In	4 2 5 5 8 5 4 7 5 – 45	**90**

Morris
Out	5 5 6 6 6 6 5 3 4 – 46	
In	4 4 5 6 7 4 6 8 5 – 49	**95**

Park
Out	6 5 5 4 7 4 6 4 3 – 44	
In	4 3 5 5 7 4 5 7 5 – 45	**89**

The second round had started at 2:00pm, and after watching Martin make a good start, Strath hit a nervy drive that sliced onto sand (it would have been out-of-bounds today). His second went into the burn, which he played out of, managing to scramble for a five. Meanwhile, his partner Dow, who had played the hole without difficulty, three-putted from close in for a six—a familiar story to a lot of club golfers in match play. Dow must have struggled after that, for he failed to record a score. Davie Strath wasn't having an easy time of it either, missing "a difficult short putt at the third but holing a 20-yarder at the fifth to save par."

On the way back he drove into a whin at the 10th on the left, but "played out beautifully and laid up stiff on his third shot." He was bunkered at the 12th. He hit whins again off the 13th tee down the right, and again down the left, hacked out and then played a master stroke onto the green and holed in five. His round became even more eventful when, after playing two good shots at the 14th, it is recorded that, "he struck Mr Hutton, upholsterer, who was playing out (presumably on the 5th fairway), on the forehead and he fell to the ground. We are glad to say that although Mr Hutton was stunned he was able to walk home."

After that incident Strath could only manage sixes at the 15th and 16th. By the time he stepped onto the 17th tee the crowd had increased by several hundred. He drove straight in to the station park but played a good shot out and over onto the fairway. He played his iron with a following wind, up toward the green, but, unbeknown to him, it struck someone on the foot while they were putting out, which stopped the ball from going onto the road. He holed out for five. Objections were made, but Strath seemed unaware of what had happened. Needing a five down the last to win, he was lucky to make six with the gallery surrounding him and impeding his every move.

The Result

Before the official announcement the committee met to discuss disqualification, but no decision was made, as the Strath incident wasn't the only one in an unruly and disorganised day's play. The Championship was eventually declared a tie between Martin and Strath, and it was decided that 18 holes would be played on the Monday to decide the outcome and the prize money (£10 and £5) but "under protest."

Davie Strath declined to play at all under such a condition. A large number sympathised with him in what was considered an unfortunate and unsatisfactory outcome. If he had played and won, would the committee then have disqualified him? While giving up the cup and the differ-

"Prince Leopold plays himself into the office as the Captain of the R&A, by driving off the first tee at the end of the Autumn Meeting."

ence in prize money, Strath was willing just to play for the honour of it. Poor Davie was not to figure again in an Open, for by 1879, dying of consumption, he left for Australia in the hope of restoring his health. His brother Andrew, who had represented St Andrews in the first Open and who won in 1865, died young of the same affliction.

Bob Martin walked the course on Monday and was declared the champion golfer of the year. Willie Park was third despite his poor first round. Tom Morris, Bob Thompson of Elie, and Mungo Park all tied for fourth place and had to play off on Monday morning to sort out the rest of the prize money. Thompson and Park played a round together, recording scores of 94 and 96.

Meanwhile Tom Morris played Willie Park in a Challenge behind them, which was halved—with both carding 92—but Morris was declared fourth in the Championship, picking up £4 in prize money.

Believe it or not, following this game was another 18-hole match between Gourlay, Kirk, and Paxton to decide on 7th and 8th place and to win £1. Paxton, from Musselburgh, must have thought the better of it and went home on Sunday.

Bob Martin, the declared winner, was a registered caddie and part-time clubmaker with Tom Morris. He was known as "the herdie laddie" because he had been a shepherd locally during the winter months.

Young Tom Morris with The Challenge Belt in 1870.

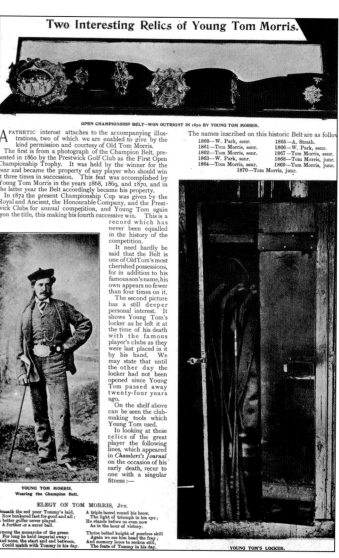

Article from *Golf Illustrated* in the 1890s.

Studio portrait of Prince Leopold, taken by Thomas Rodger who produced a photographic album, a gift from the town to its royal guest, recording all the memorable events during the week of his installation as Captain of the Royal and Ancient in 1876.

A full-size portrait of John Whyte Melville, Captain of the Society of St Andrews Golfers in 1823, hangs in the main room of the R&A Clubhouse, painted by Sir Francis Grant (also a member of the club).

After much altercation, the ill-fated David Strath refused to play off with Bob Martin to resolve the outcome of what had become a bitter dispute and so lost his chance of winning the 1876 Open.

Thomas Hodge, a prominent member of the R&A, sketched this colourful gathering during the Autumn Meeting of 1862.

Below left: The Championship Medal of 1876.

Below: Bob Martin, the controversial winner of the 1876 Open.

RULES
REGARDING
PAY AND DISCIPLINE OF CADDIES,
ADOPTED BY
THE ROYAL AND ANCIENT GOLF CLUB OF ST. ANDREWS,
At a Special General Meeting of the Club, held on 3rd February, 1875.

I.—All Caddies shall be Enrolled,—none being admitted under 13 years of age.

II.—Members of the Club shall employ only Enrolled Caddies.

III.—A List of Enrolled Caddies shall be placed in the Club Hall, and also in the Clubmakers' Shops.

IV.—Caddies shall be divided into Two Classes, according to skill or age, and their services shall be rated as follows:—

First Class Caddies.—Eighteenpence for First Round, and One Shilling for each following Round, or part of Round.

Second Class Caddies.—One Shilling for First Round, and Sixpence for each following Round, or part of Round.

V.—No Caddy, unless previously engaged, can refuse to carry for a Member, under penalty of suspension for a stated time.

VI.—Names of suspended or disqualified Caddies shall be posted.

VII.—Complaints regarding Caddies shall be made through the Keeper of the Green to the Green Committee, who shall award an adequate penalty.

VIII.—The penalty shall be awarded by not less than two of the Green Committee.

IX.—The Keeper of the Green shall have charge of the Caddies, and Members shall apply to him when in want of a Caddy.

X.—Members are particularly urged to report all cases of misconduct on the part of the Caddies, whether during their time of service or otherwise,—such as incivility, bad language, abusing the Green, or any other form of misdemeanour—which may merit censure or penalty.

XI.—Tom Morris shall be Keeper of the Green, and Superintendent of the Caddies.

Printed rules concerning the employment of local caddies were distributed to all members of the R&A at their Spring Meeting of 1875.

"Teeing off midway through the major transitions of the game. From lum hats to bowler hats, from cricket caps to flat caps, red velvet to tweed, goose-necked clubs to brassies, feather balls to gutties, and Autumn Meetings to Open Championships."

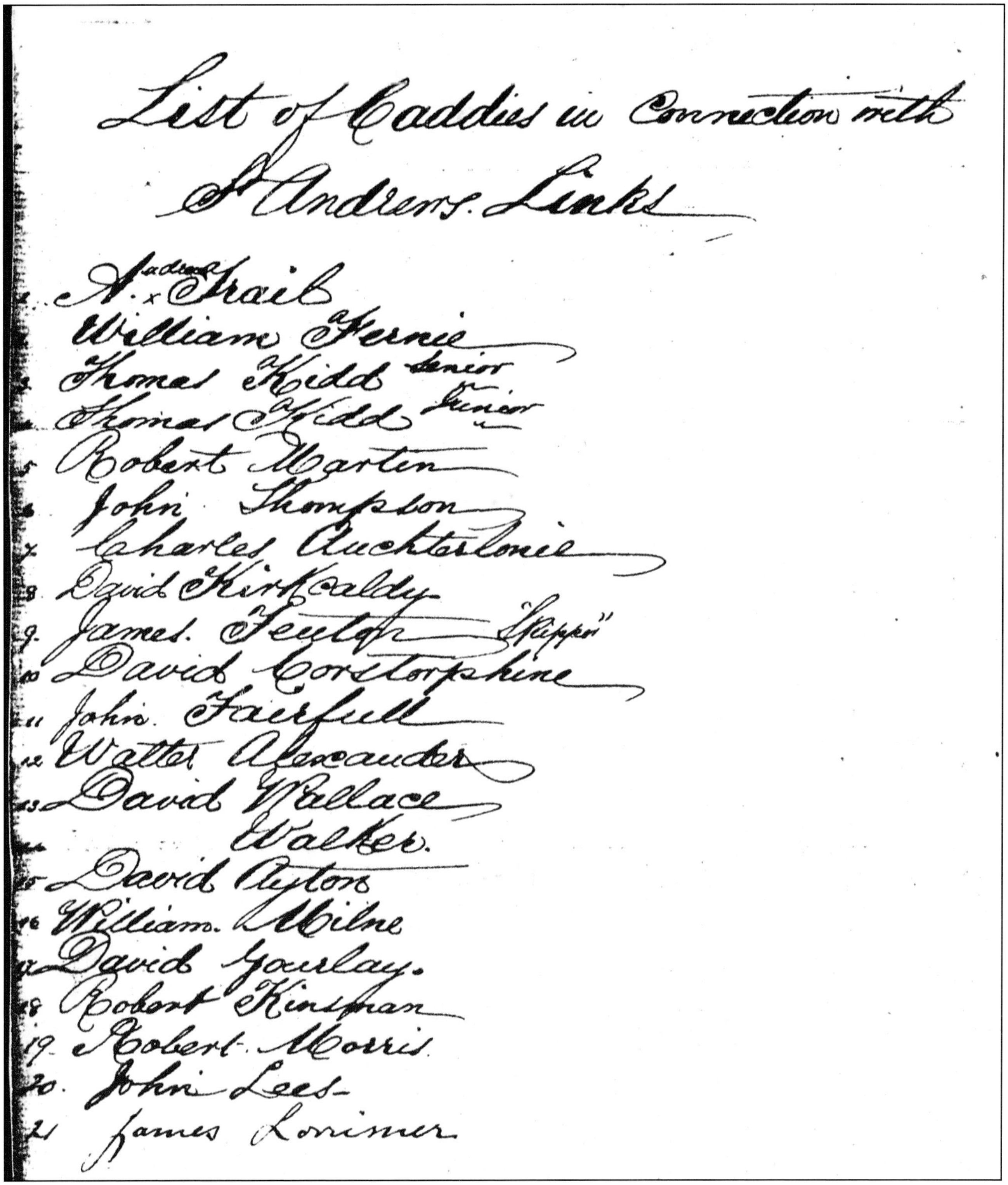

List of Caddies in Connection with

St Andrews Links

1. A. Traill
2. William Fernie
3. Thomas Kidd senior
4. Thomas Kidd junior
5. Robert Martin
6. John Thompson
7. Charles Auchterlonie
8. David Kirkaldy
9. James Seaton "Skipper"
10. David Corstorphine
11. John Fairfull
12. Walter Alexander
13. David Wallace
14. Walker
15. David Ayton
16. William Milne
17. David Gourlay
18. Robert Kinsman
19. Robert Morris
20. John Lees
21. James Lorimer

This list of registered caddies in 1876 includes three Open Champions:

No. 2 William Fernie, who was to win at Musselburgh in 1883.

No. 4 Thomas Kidd Jr, the first winner at St Andrews in 1873.

No. 5 Robert Martin, double winner at St Andrews in 1876 and 1885.

4TH OCTOBER, 1879: "THE WEATHER WAS VERY FINE—THE LINKS IN ITS BEST CONDITION."

Below is a list of all the competitors as was posted the evening before the tournament—23 pairings. At the time this was considered "an exceptionally large muster" for the championship. The list read:

James Kirk, St Andrews, and G. Honeyman, Golf Hotel, St Andrews
Mr Fitzroy Boothby and Mr J.H. Blackwell, R&A
Tom Kidd and Andrew Kirkaldy, St Andrews and John Kirkaldy, St Andrews
T. Annandale, Glasgow, and Jim Allen, Westward Ho
Smith Cambridge and Willie Fernie, St Andrews
Stewart and Mr R. Armit
Kinsman, St Andrews, and Ben Sayers, Leith
Mr Henry Lamb and Henry Wilson, London
David Ayton, St Andrews, and Mr A.W. Smith, Glasgow
Dr Argyll Robertson, Edinburgh, and J.O.F. Morris, St Andrews
Mr D. Lundie and Tom Dunn, Wimbledon
George Strath, Glasgow, and D. Corstorphine
Bob Dow, Montrose, and Walter Gourlay, Perth
W. Doleman, Glasgow, and G. Paxman, Musselburgh
Bob Ferguson, North Berwick, and James Rennie
J. "Skipper" Fenton, and J. Manzie, St Andrews
Mr W. Goff and Mr J. Cameron
Jamie Anderson, St Andrews, and Mr Thomson White, Edinburgh
Davie Anderson, St Andrews, and George Lowe, Hoylake
W. Grieg and Tom Kirk, St Andrews
Bob Kirk and Bob Martin, St Andrews
Tom Morris, St Andrews, and George Grant, Leith

Tom Morris played last, as he was starting off all the matches.

Game 19: Jamie Anderson teed off at 11:30. "Anderson commenced operations with a splendid swipe." He played a fine, steady game with what was acknowledged as an exceedingly good score of 84. Had he holed his chances he would have stormed away from the field, but his score was still the best round of the day.

Anderson

Out	5 5 4 5 6 5 5 4 3 4 – 41	
In	4 4 4 5 6 5 6 5 5 5 5 – 43	**84**

Despite a near disaster at the 16th—with Anderson in the Principal's Nose (a bunker) off the tee and Mr White, his playing partner, on the railway line—they both managed fives. Mr White, relieved by such an escape, promptly took an eight at the 17th and faded from the picture.

Bob Ferguson—who had beaten Jamie Anderson that week—had a good start, but "quite damaged his reputation at the Long Hole, where he came to grief among bunkers and rough grass."

J.O.F. Morris, Old Tom's youngest son, played a good game but ill luck seemed to pursue him throughout. The bounce of the ball was a major factor in scoring on hard, rutted fairways. A ball could shoot from the centre of a fairway at right angles into trouble—severe trouble.

Jim Allen from Westward Ho played "a capital game" outward on both rounds in 41 and 38 respectively, but fell away on the homeward journey with 47 and 46.

With a second round of 85, Jamie Anderson was declared the winner by three shots. He thus claimed the distinction—as did Young Tom Morris before him—of

Autumnal shadows emphasize the severity of catching one of the three bunkers known as "the Principal's Nose," off of the sixteenth tee.

winning three successive Championships, having won in Musselburgh in 1877 and in Prestwick in 1878.

Playoffs

On Monday morning Andrew Kirkaldy and Jamie Allen, who had tied for second place, played off. Kirkaldy won an extremely close match, 91 to 92. Allen then had to turn round and play a challenge against J.O.F. Morris, and again was beaten by one shot, 87 to 88.

Did all who tied play off, as in 1873 and 1876? If so, J.O.F. Morris, Tom Dunn, and W. Gourlay would have had to play together to decide 8th, 9th, and 10th place; Rennie, Fernie, and Hugh Kirkaldy for 11th, 12th, and 13th; and Annandale and Ayton for the last pound.

There was no respite for the few professional players lucky enough to attract a big crowd on the following days. For example, "Another Great Professional Golf Match" was set up between Anderson and Allen. Two hundred pounds—one hundred pounds over the match as a whole and twenty-five pounds on each of four greens—St Andrews, Prestwick, Hoylake, and Westward Ho. This was big money, for there was only forty-five pounds to divide for the succeeding top 14 players in the Championship. Anderson, who had won the first prize of ten pounds, was five holes up in this challenge after the first round at St Andrews. Allen got two back in the afternoon, but Anderson pocketed twenty-five pounds—and off they went to Prestwick.

Originally portable, Victorian bathing huts used to be wheeled down to the tide line on the West Sands to protect a lady's modesty from straying eyes, when in flimsy swimsuits, all shapes and sizes, took the plunge. In turn, one of those huts was converted to a starter's box and pulled onto the Old Course every morning during the 1880s and '90s. The ballot for the day and a list of available caddies were posted. A tripod was placed to the side of the box and from a hatch the starter hung tin plates numbered for the order of play.

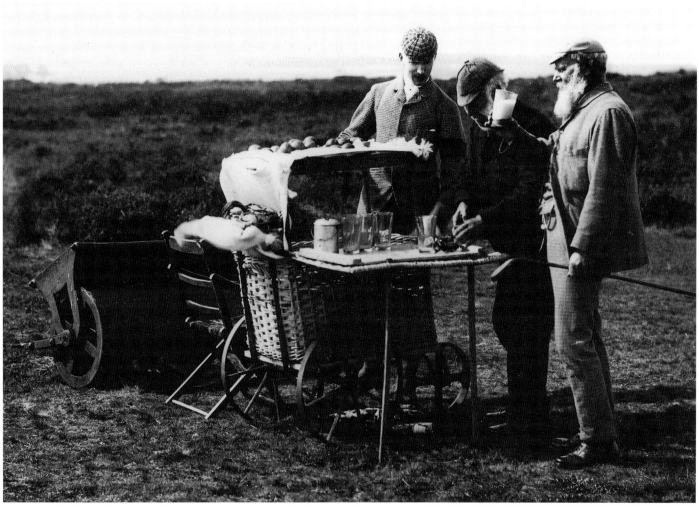

Above: Tom Morris on the right and Daw Anderson in the centre. Daw Anderson was the father of Jamie, who had caddied for Tom Morris in the 1840s. The ginger beer stand, which Daw manned, was wheeled out to the fourth hole (named "Ginger Beer") and provided refreshments in the form of half lemons, ginger beer, and milk. A bottle of gin was hidden away in a leather hatbox for the convenience of the occasionally traumatised Royal and Ancient Golf Club member having a bad round.

Taking refreshment at the ginger beer stand. Peter Anderson (seated), representing St Andrews University, won the British Amateur Championship in 1893.

Left: Jamie Anderson, winner of three consecutive Championships, achieved the third in 1879 on his home course in St Andrews. Anderson did not defend his title for a fourth time at Musselburgh in 1880, saying that it had been too short notice for him by the time the date of the Championship was announced.

From first light in a busy summer, golfers queue, hopeful of a game by being first in line for start of play at 7:00am. Having missed out on the ballot (the official draw for tee times made at 2:00pm on the previous day), it is their only chance of playing the Old Course by "making up a four ball" or hoping for a last minute cancellation.

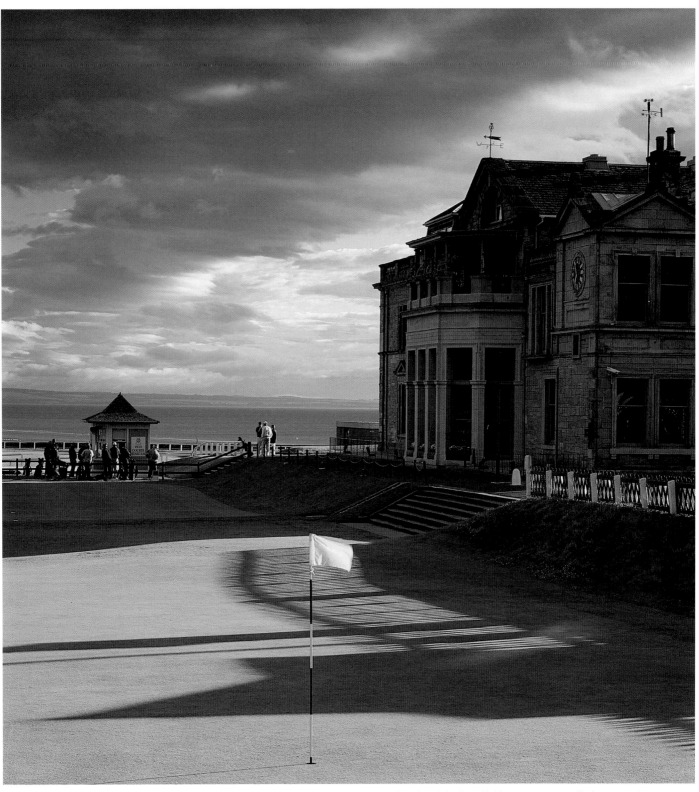

Long shadows creep across the eighteenth green as play gets underway as the stately Royal and Ancient Clubhouse oversees all players as they start their rounds.

1882

"ON SATURDAY 30TH OF SEPTEMBER THE ANNUAL GOLF CHAMPIONSHIP AS USUAL BROUGHT THE ROYAL AND ANCIENT GOLF CLUB MEETING TO A CLOSE. IT WAS FITTING THAT AFTER THE GENTLEMEN OF THE CLUB HAD EXPENDED THEIR STRENGTH ON THE THREE PRECEDING DAYS THE PROFESSIONAL PLAYERS SHOULD HAVE THEIR INNINGS ALSO. THE DAY WAS ONE OF THE BEST OF THE SEASON—NOT TOO BRIGHT SUNSHINE— WITH A MODERATE BREEZE, WHICH DID NOT AFFECT THE FLIGHT OF THE BALL."

Twenty pairings started at 10:00 am They were described as the main Scottish pros—a few crack amateurs and three English greens—Hoylake, Warrington, and Wimbledon. Through subscription nine prizes would be played for— twelve pounds to the winner and decreasing to nine pounds, seven, six, five, three, two, and one, with fifteen shillings as an extra prize for the best inward nine. It was announced that the trophy would be retained in the principal club of the district from which the winner came.

Despite there being eight St Andreans in the first nine matches, the crowd hung back until game ten for two past St Andrews winners—Jamie Anderson and Bob Martin—in the expectation that they would at least witness steady golf. They weren't to be disappointed. Anderson started with six fives in a row, with four, three, three, to be out in 40. Despite sevens at the 13th and 14th, he got back in 47. Martin, just as steady, though out in 43, went well enough until the 17th, where he too put a dreaded 7 on his card. He finished in 89, two shots behind Anderson.

Mr Fitz Boothby of the R&A proudly handed in his card of 86. He had gone out in 41, just as he had on the Wednesday when winning his club's gold medal.

Bob Ferguson from Musselburgh, who had won the last two Opens, was paired with local man David Ayton. They had been close behind Anderson and Martin. Considering the pressure Ferguson was under, he started like a true champion, going out in 40 to match Anderson. Ferguson started back four, three, four, to be only three over fours. Would this cause a sensation and be the first score under 80 in the Championship? No—although he came back in 43, yet again the last 6 holes (as shown with the leading scores in 1876) pulled him back. The prize for the best inward nine was to be shared, with a score of 42 by Fernie, Park, Martin, and Lowe. It would be hardly enough to buy a packet of peanuts today.

Ferguson's first round of 83 was four shots better than anyone could match over the two rounds, and an 88 saw him win by that margin from Willie Fernie.

Bob Ferguson—like Anderson—had now won the Claret Jug three times in a row. He nearly claimed a fourth con-secutive title the next year, to emulate Young Tom's feat. On his home course at Musselburgh, having tied with Willie Fernie, he lost in the 18-hole playoff when Fernie beat him by sinking a long putt for a two.

Ferguson's game was never as sharp again, and he stopped playing soon after that, though partly due to a recurring illness. He went back to caddying, which he'd done most of his life, and, despite ill health, lived on another 37 years.

A deep pot bunker, lying in wait to the right of "hell," leads onto the steep ridge protecting the fourteenth green.

Bob Ferguson in his prime (right) and caddying in later life (above).

In 1882, a small hardback book, "The Golfers Handbook," carried a dozen adverts relating to golfers mainly from St Andrews although the back cover was sponsored by The Scottish Widows Fund. Note the advert for the Royal Hotel, "Omnibus (horse and carriage) attends all trains"—as did the caddies lying in wait to grab a gentleman's clubs in the hope of a daily booking during the duration of his stay.

The Holes

1st — Burn — 370 yards, par 4

Despite the generous width of the first and eighteenth fairways—not a bunker to be seen—teeing off in the shadow of the Royal and Ancient Golf Club is still an intimidating drive. With the length most professionals hit the ball nowadays, the Burn comes into play both right and left. The approach shot across the Swilken Burn is inhibiting, and many a ball has even spun back into it from the green for a demoralising "pick and drop" at the start of a round. The next 16 holes will have—among other treacherous hazards—112 bunkers waiting for you!

2nd — Dyke — 411 yards, par 4

Like most holes on the way out, trouble awaits you down the right. Cheape's Bunker, left centre, is there to catch a good drive. Bobby Jones was in almost perfect control of his game in winning in 1927—apart from catching this bunker three times in his four championship rounds. Depending on the pin placement, steep undulations defending the green make for an awkward shot.

3rd — Cartgate — 400 yards, par 4

One of the easier birdie chances if the weather conditions are favourable. Drive right of centre to ease the pressure of possibly landing in Cartgate Bunker, which guards the left side of the green on a lofted approach. (Cartgate was named after a cart track, which crossed the fairways in days gone by). There is a subtle small ridge just in front of the green, which can cause a ball to dramatically kick off at right angles if it is slightly short. The green itself can be a difficult one to read.

4th — Ginger Beer — 463 yards, par 4

The toughest par 4 of the outward nine, where a decision has to be made whether to hit straight down a narrow gap or drive left of the grassy ridge, centre. A large "hump" obscures the flag on what is normally a long iron into the green. Named Ginger Beer—a wicker basket on wheels was pushed out onto this hole every day by "a respectable caddie"–the first "refreshment tent" on a golf course!

Next page: 5th Hole — O' Cross — 564 yards, par 5

Beware of the Seven Sisters!–a group of bunkers awaiting a drive slightly off line down the right. Another two hazards, The Spectacles, look deep—and are, as they dominate either side of the steep ridge just short of a big dip leading up to the largest green in the world. Sharing its status with the thirteenth, from front to back it is nearly 100 yards. It was considered "the finest surface in the land" as far back as 1850.

6th — Heathery — 416 yards, par 4

Named originally because of the texture of its green—not its fairway! A blind shot over whin, avoiding six bunkers right and The Coffins and Nicks to the left. The approach is fairly straightforward apart from a dip in front of the green.

7th — High — 372 yards, par 4

This hole shares a very long snake-like green with the eleventh. The flag is not visible from the tee, but thick whins, protecting the right-hand side of the fairway, certainly are. A good drive with a carry of 240 yards will see you over this trouble or, again from the tee, aim slightly right of a large hummock in the centre of the fairway. A big bunker, "Shell," protects the front of an undulating green.

10th — Bobby Jones — 380 yards, par 4

"About Turn" for the tenth, which is similar to the ninth but a trickier approach, with a ridge protecting the front and a fall away to the right, catches a timid shot. Having been lengthened recently, it is not the driveable hole of old, when Arnold Palmer attacked the green in every round during the Centenary Open. A request by the Town Council to name this hole "Bobby Jones" was approved after his death in 1971.

Opposite top: 8th — Short — 178 yards, par 3

Turning round, the backdrop to this hole is the dramatic skyline of the town with its prominent towers and steeples. Although the bottom of the flag is not visible, it is a fairly straightforward shot on a calm day (which are few and far between!). Jock Hutchison holed in one in the opening round of the 1921 Open, and Ben Crenshaw was another to do so in 1984.

Opposite bottom: 9th — End — 356 yards, par 4

Apart from two bunkers well up the fairway, "Boase's" and "End Hole," which split the ninth from the tenth and a layer of inhospitable heather running the length of the left-hand side, this is an easier birdie hole. Players are looking for a possible sub-par score playing round the loop (the seventh to the twelfth) before they face the last six holes.

11th — High — 172 yards, par 3

If you hit either of the two bunkers—"Strath," normally guarding the flag or "Hill" to the left—then you're in trouble! Bobby Jones tore up his card in the 1921 Open after three stabs in "Hill." Payne Stewart managed to par the eleventh from a seemingly impossible position during the last round of the '90 Open; trying to catch Faldo. He played back up from a hollow, having hit through the green, and managed to stop the ball by the flag, which was positioned near the bottom of a slippery slope. In fact, if you get above the hole when the green is quick, just by nudging the ball, or merely setting it in motion, it may well run all the way off and back down the fairway!

Strath Bunker on the front right of the green.

12th — Heathery — 316 yards, par 4

Most top professionals are now looking to drive this hole. The green was first hit in one by Craig Wood, runner-up in the 1933 Open, and again by fellow American Sam Snead, on his way to winning the Open in 1946. Fifteen yards short of the green lies a small, but deep, bunker. A sharp steep slope protects the flag. This is where the traditional St Andrews pitch and run with a five iron, "down the shaft," would come in useful as the approach shot.

13th — Hole 'O Cross — 429 yards, par 4

Many a good score has been ruined on the way in after driving into one of the ominously named bunkers, "Coffins," in the centre of the fairway. The second shot, providing you're in play, is equally challenging, having to fly the ball all the way to the hole and avoid an unpredictable bounce at the front of this huge green. In the first Opens played on the Old Course, scoring proved difficult from here in, with an average of level sixes!

14th — Long — 567 yards, par 5

Out-of-bounds to the right and a group of bunkers, "The Beardies," to the left will catch you if you stray from the centre of the fairway. "The Elysian Fields"—so named as it was the only respite you got on the original course (in the reverse of how it is played today) before the first Opens were played at St Andrews. To avoid "Hell" (bunker), hit down the fifth fairway because they've added even more height to the face just recently. The mighty Jack Nicklaus, like many famous names before him, came to grief in it during the '95 Open. Having managed to avoid all this trouble, there is still a tricky shot into the green with a steep slope shielding the hole.

15th — Cartgate — 459 yards, par 4

When lining up on the fifteenth tee, "just aim on the right hand steeple!" (one of the seven landmarks on the town's skyline)...which stands out in the distance down the centre of the fairway in a gap between two humps, 290 yards away. Like the sixteenth, this championship tee has been lengthened recently for the Open. The second shot has to be flighted straight to the flag, as typical links "humps and bumps" will catch you at the entrance to the green.

16th — Corner of the Dyke — 426 yards, par 4

Out-of-bounds all the way to the green on the right (the old railway line) with a group of three driveable bunkers named "The Principal's Nose" down the middle. The percentage shot is to pick a spot to the left of the "Nose!"—but this lengthens the hole and brings "Wig" bunker, sunk into a bank at the front of the green into play, left of the flag. In 1905, in the final round, James Braid drove into "The Principal's Nose," then whacked a long shot onto the railway line—as he had at the previous hole (it was not O.B. at that time). He still won the Open by five shots.

17th — Road — 461 yards, par 4

The seventeenth, one of the most difficult par 4s in the world, was in fact played as a par 5 up until the 1964 Open. A demanding tee shot has to be negotiated over the "Black Sheds" (originally used for storing hickory) within the grounds of the Old Course Hotel. Aim for the "O" on "Course" on the sign "Old Course Hotel," preferably with a touch of draw, and this will take you to the middle of the fairway, where your long iron will have to be extremely accurate.

Two problems lie in wait for you around the green. The first is how to avoid the infamous Road Hole bunker of "Nakajima's," as it has been cruelly known since the Japanese contender's trauma in the 1978 Open. It seems to attract like a magnet, with the steep contour at the front of the green enticing the ball into its sandy grave. Nick Faldo took no chances and sensibly played the seventeenth as a par 5 and laid up short in all four rounds of the 1990 Open, still managing to finish 17 under! The second problem is how to hold the ball on the green and prevent it from rolling down on the road, or worse, bounding over against the wall.

18th — Tom Morris — 354 yards, par 4

Hit a long drive on the line of the Royal and Ancient Clubhouse clock and acknowledge the ecstatic crowd as you walk across the Swilken Bridge and down the last fairway, like all the great names before you. A tricky shot avoiding the Valley of Sin may await you but, like Constantino Rocca in the 1995 Open, have no fear of it! Hole a 15-footer with a big swing right to left to win in a new championship record of 18 under par to beat Tiger Woods by a shot...now dream on!

1885

ON THE SATURDAY OF THE CHAMPIONSHIP (3RD OCTOBER) THE LOCAL PAPER, *THE ST ANDREWS CITIZEN*, SIMPLY REPORTED, "A STIFF BREEZE." MEANWHILE, ONE WEEK LATER, IN ONE OF THE FIRST NATIONAL REPORTS OF THE EVENT, *THE DAILY MAIL* TOOK A VERY AGGRESSIVE ATTITUDE TOWARD THE EVENT BY SAYING:

"The great golfers' meeting at St Andrews is just over. Why has the season of the equinoctial gales been chosen for this contest by a club, which is Royal and Ancient?

Furious and tyrannical weather has not even the advantage of keeping women away from the scene. Out they come in Mackintoshes, ulsters, and deerstalking caps in their legions.

How can we attribute such a terrible defeat of gentlemen by players in this late championship?

The differentia, on good judicial authority is stated thus—'The gentleman player wears gloves. The professional does not wear gloves—and he spits on his hands.'"

Mr Charles Grace—a local lawyer who took over from his father after his 43-year stint as Honorary Secretary of the R&A that year—would surely have been concerned about such a hostile report. The prize money for the Open—of which half was donated by the Club and the other half by gentlemen attending the Autumn Meeting—was not placed in jeopardy by such a conflict on this occasion. This tradition would have to change as the tournament progressed. I doubt if the members in the Autumn Meeting nowadays would be able or willing to find the £851,000 for the total purse of 1995!

The Open was gaining attention, for during that golfing week the St Andrews Post Office telegraphed out 11,000 words of press for the newspapers.

Fifty-six entered in a strong field, weakened only by the nonappearance of Jamie Anderson, Bob Ferguson, and Willie Dunn. The Simpson brothers from Carnoustie were much fancied, Jack being the defending champion after his win at Prestwick. The "gloved gentlemen" Mr Laidlay and Mr Balfour, who were paired together, had been playing against each other all of that week. Both had plenty of backers, Laidlay having won the R&A Gold Medal on Wednesday. But it was Mr Horace Hutchison, a great amateur player and writer of the game, who finished best—seven shots off the leader.

Despite a brave challenge by Archie Simpson as the wind got stronger in the afternoon, Bob Martin had played a steady, careful game and emerged the victor for the second time at St Andrews. He was loudly applauded all the way down the last fairway. He was five shots better than in his last victory, in 1876.

Although still caddying and making clubs with Tom Morris, he had become the first double winner at St Andrews. Later the feat would also be accomplished by James Braid, J.H. Taylor, and Jack Nicklaus.

Rose Bay willowherb, ragwort, and whin react to the wind and create a moving foreground for the shared third and fifteenth green.

On the largest green in the world, the flagpole, exposed to a summer gale-force wind, bends to the breaking point.

Below: Jack Simpson representing Carnoustie was the pre-Open favourite, having won by four shots on the new 18 holes of Prestwick the year before. Although finishing fourth equal, three shots behind the winner, it was one of his five golfing brothers, Archie, who fared better on the day, being runner-up to Bob Martin by a shot.

Illustration of spectators around the last green with flags hanging limply from the original mast of the "Cutty Sark."

Below: A lineup of competitors outside the Prestwick Golf Club at the previous year's Open. The well-known bearded face of Tom Morris in the front row is flanked by Willie Park Jr on his right, double winner in 1887 and 1889 (son of Old Tom's great adversary and first winner of the Open), and on his left, Andrew Kirkaldy, runner-up to his own brother in 1891 at St Andrews, and future Honorary Professional to the Royal and Ancient.

Despite being a double winner of the Open at St Andrews, Bob Martin spent the next 20 years as a clubmaker with Tom Morris. Martin is second on the left, with Old Tom leaning out of the top window and his youngest and only surviving son, J.O.F., who ran the business at the turn of the century, in the doorway.

This photograph of a competitor playing the fifth in the 1885 Open shows how rough the texture of "The Hazards" still were, compared with the group of manicured bunkers, "The Seven Sisters," that await you there now.

Horace Hutchinson was the leading "gentlemen golfer" (amateur) seven shots behind Martin. He was an outspoken writer on the game. In the following year he wrote of the proposed formation of the Ladies' Golf Union that, "Women never have and never can unite to push any scheme to success. They are bound to fall out and quarrel on the smallest or no provocation; they are built that way! Tears will bedew, if wigs do not bestew the green. Constitutionally and physically they are unfitted for golf. Temperamentally the strain will be too great for them."

1888

WITH THE TOURNAMENT POSTPONED BY A WEEK AND THE MAJORITY OF THE R&A GEN-TLEMEN GONE FROM THE AUTUMN MEETING, THE PRIZE MONEY DROPPED—THROUGH LACK OF SUBSCRIPTION, CERTAINLY NOT THROUGH LACK OF INTEREST. ALTHOUGH THE CLUB HAD ONLY MANAGED TO RAISE £2 FROM ITS MEMBERSHIP, IT ADDED ANOTHER £20, WHICH WOULD AT LEAST ENSURE THE FUTURE OF THE OPEN. THE TROPHY, MEDAL, AND £8 WENT TO JACK BURNS, DESCRIBED AS, "A STRAPPING YOUNG FELLOW." BURNS WAS AT THAT TIME GREENKEEPER AND PROFESSIONAL TO THE WARWICKSHIRE GOLF CLUB BUT A BORN AND BRED ST ANDREAN.

By winning, Jack Burns had suddenly gained notoriety, though seeing his form over the last summer you would have had no hesitation in putting him in the first rank. He was a powerful and straight driver. Later in life he was often quoted as saying, "I haven't been off the line for years." (His last 20 years he spent working on the railway.)

As they said of Tom Kidd when he unexpectedly won the first St Andrews Open, the local paper also said of Jack Burns that, "his short game was deficient and could with practice be improved. On that inhospitable day it was his putting and the pretty way he handled his iron that won for him."

On that day the wind had been blowing strongly from the northwest (left-to-right and slightly against on the way out) which pushed the ball toward the trouble. Turning round, the right-to-left wind proved easier, as is indicated by the top three cards. Many of the fancied players couldn't cope with the conditions, but Mr Leslie Balfour, a gentleman golfer, had what was recorded as an excep-tional day, finishing fourth but only two shots off the lead. Davie Anderson Jr (brother of past winner Jamie) was the first man ever to break 40 on the inward half of his first round. Jack Burns—despite dropping four shots on the first three holes back in the final round—steadied up and believed he had won, as did Ben Sayers of North Berwick.

First Round

Jack Burns

Out	5 5 6 5 7 6 5 4 3 — 47	
In	5 3 4 5 4 5 4 5 5 — 40	**87**

Ben Sayers

Out	5 5 5 5 7 5 3 5 5 — 45	
In	5 4 4 5 4 4 5 5 4 — 40	**85**

Early morning sunlight on the longest day casts a shadow across "Scholars" bunker.

Davie Anderson Jr
Out   5 6 7 5 7 5 5 4 3 – 47
In   4 4 4 4 5 5 5 5 4 4 – 39   **86**

Second Round
Jack Burns
Out   6 6 4 5 5 5 4 4 3 – 42
In   6 4 5 5 5 4 4 6 4 – 43   **85**   172

Ben Sayers
Out   5 5 5 5 8 6 6 3 3 – 46
In   5 4 4 5 5 4 4 6 4 – 41   **87**   172

Davie Anderson Jr
Out   5 5 5 5 7 5 5 5 3 – 45
In   5 3 3 6 5 5 4 6 4 – 41   **86**   172

A tie was declared, but on the cards, being checked by a Mr Everard, it was found that Burns had gone out in the first 9 on 46, not the 47 shown on the previous page. With the inconsistency of the scoring, it would have been an easy mistake to make. As the crowd milled about the last green, wondering if a play-off would be set for the following Monday, an announcement was made from Tom Morris's shop that Burns had become the World Champion Golfer. The crowd—although slightly confused—cheered heartily!

Jack Burns in later life retired from the railway and went back to "the caddyin." Posing here with a piece of abrasive emery paper in his hand which he used to shine up the head of the gentleman's niblick and keep rust at bay in a time-honoured tradition.

Below: Crowd control was a reoccurring problem at Open Championships with spectators breathing down the necks of the players—even in the middle of the fairways. In this photograph only the burn is keeping them off the green!

With 16 names on the Claret Jug by 1888, they were rapidly running out of room for the annual hand-engraving on the trophy, so Jack Burns was relegated to the underside of the spout. A silver-collared plinth would soon have to be used to accommodate the Open's future winners.

A crowd on the last green.

1891

THE CHAMPIONSHIP WAS SWITCHED TO THE TUESDAY AFTER THE AUTUMN MEETING.

ENTRIES CLOSED ON SATURDAY THE 3RD OF OCTOBER. THIS WAS TO BE THE LAST OF

THIS OLD FORMAT, FOR THINGS WERE TO CHANGE.

There were 73 competitors, but of those there were 10 late entrants, about whom some of the committee and several professionals had complained. The amateur players, on the whole, had no objection. It was a major blow for Tom Vardon (whose brother, Harry, was to become the record six-time winner of the Open) and George Lowe, because they had missed the closing date after a long trip up from St Anne's-on-Sea. Three had also come over from North Berwick, and David Brown, the champion at Musselburgh in 1886, and representing the Malvern Club, had arrived late from across the border.

An emergency meeting was called on Monday evening at 10:00 pm. It was attended by some of the late entrants, a few professionals already drawn, and the committee. The R&A committee were not at all intimidated by this lineup but no decision was made until the players left the meeting. The committee then decided not to admit the late entrants to the competition.

Looking at the results the next day, the late entrants all played anyway! David Brown was the only one of the banned players to be in contention—finishing seventh—and should have won one pound. Although recording and posting his scores of 88 and 86, no money is entered after his name. Ben Sayers, two shots behind, got the money instead.

Apart from challenge matches prior to the Championship there is no mention of a practice round in any Open up until this time. The weather was described as favourable on Monday's round, but on the next day of the Championship proper a heavy rain set in, and, although it cleared in the afternoon, the greens were left in "a soppy condition."

Mr John Ball, the defending champion, had been the first amateur to win an Open—and a foreigner at that! (He was English.) He came to grief during the first round. At "The Burn Hole"—which had just been renamed "The Road Hole"—the ball had in fact hit the road and become stuck in a deep rut. He took an 11, for a 94. He then took 11 shots off his afternoon's round to equal the total score of the eventual winner, Hugh Kirkaldy, who had two 83s.

Despite the weather, a large crowd followed Hugh Kirkaldy and his partner, Mr Carmichael, representing St Andrews University—two dashing young men with very full swings. Hugh played well, apart from a seven at the long 14th and a six at the 17th. In the afternoon he bogied and double bogied the two short holes, but managed to keep a six off his card. It was the first card ever recorded with no more than a five on it. Out in 38, he made nine fives in a row on the way back!

As in past Championships, the last six holes were a real struggle for most. Willie Fernie, representing Troon— going exceptionally well in the heavy weather—was only two over fours standing on the 13th tee. This created great excitement and an instant crowd, but he finished with five consecutive sixes, saving face with a four at the last and a round of 84. He tied with Hugh Kirkaldy's brother Andrew for second place. Andrew Kirkaldy had already been runner-up to Willie Park Jr two years before at Musselburgh. He was the more fancied of the two and was

"Short Hole" bunker guards the eighth green.

to be in contention in most of the major tournaments for many years. Andrew, or "Andra" as he was known, was to become the Honorary Professional to the R&A, replacing Tom Morris, and was featured as The Starter for the Tournament—when played for in St Andrews—up until 1933. Despite finishing 75 in the play-off, he won by two shots, so the brothers achieved the unusual feat of being the winner and the runner-up, matched only by the Morrises' more unique achievement as father and son in the 1869 Open at Prestwick.

Willie Auchterlonie, who was to win in 1893, was classed as an amateur player, having just left school in St Andrews. He showed up well in getting on the "leader board" (not that there was one). Large crowds simply passed the word about on the course as to who was doing what and where, and everyone went running. Auchterlonie lost his gallery after a disastrous nine at the 14th in the second round, but eventually he tied for eighth with Mr Harold Hilton from Hoylake, who was to win the following year.

The status of the Amateur Championship—a gruelling week of match play—picked up a much bigger editorial press than the Open at that time. This was probably why a large crowd followed Mr S. Mure Fergusson, representing the Royal and Ancient, who finished his final round with a cavalier-like birdie to great cheers and finished fourth. Mr Freddie Tait got his first mention as a young captain in the Black Watch with scores of 94 and 88. He became a hugely popular figure in the game—winning two Amateur Championships in 1896 and 1898—and was in contention in the three Championships prior to his untimely death, shot in the Boer War in 1900 aged 30. Hugh Kirkaldy, after suffering a severe strain of influenza in 1896, never recovered his health, and also died young in 1900. The golfing world had yet again lost another two leading players taken in their prime.

Of the seven Opens then played at St Andrews, only Bob Ferguson had broken the monopoly of the born and bred St Andrean winners. Willie Auchterlonie, after winning at Prestwick in 1893, was to become the last home-based Scot ever to win the Championship until Paul Lawrie—106 years later. Had this been predicted at the time, it would surely have been met with total disbelief. But things were to change quite radically from that moment on…

The Winds of Change, or "Horses for Courses"

The Honourable Company of Edinburgh Golfers, who hosted the Musselburgh Open, had got restless and irritated over the condition of the course caused by just too much play on it. It was still only nine holes and falling behind as the game, the numbers playing, and the number of courses grew. Because of this, the Honourable Company moved their base to Gullane and had Muirfield laid out by Old Tom Morris and ready for play by 1891.

The first dramatic step was to introduce Muirfield as a new tournament venue in 1892 and to sideline Musselburgh. The second was to increase the play to four rounds over two days. This really did signal the end for Musselburgh. Who would be keen to play eight times round their nine holes?

Prestwick had written that year to the Royal and Ancient in the aftermath of this controversy, suggesting that the Championship be placed on a new and wider basis.

An entry fee of 10 shillings was introduced to help boost the prize money and hopefully to deter the "no hopers" from entering. Up to that point, if thick-skinned enough, anyone could enter.

The Championship at Muirfield was a success, and the three host clubs met in 1893 to "place the competition for the Open Golf Championship on a basis more commensurate with its importance than had hitherto existed." After much deliberation they decided to invite two English clubs. The first, St George's, hosted the next year's Championship at Sandwich. Royal Liverpool, where the first Muirfield winner, Harold Hilton, was based at Hoylake, was to enter the fray in 1897.

The Championship was to be run by "the delegates of the associated clubs," which seemed to work well enough up until the outbreak of World War I and the suspension of the Championship. When it reemerged in 1920 the R&A took over the entire responsibility of its running, as they have done every year since.

Back in 1893 the delegates decided that the five clubs now involved would contribute £15 annually and that the prize money should total £100, as it had done the previous year. The winner would receive £30, plus £10 for the cost of a gold medal, £20 for the runner-up, £10 for third, £7 for fourth, £5 for fifth, £4 for sixth, £3 each for seventh, eighth, and ninth, £2 for tenth and eleventh, and finally £1 for twelfth place.

The Scottish team of professionals with nonplaying captain, Tom Morris (seated), before a match against England at Lytham. Included in the team are the winner and runner-up of the 1891 Open, Hugh (far right, back row) and Andrew Kirkaldy (seated left of Tom Morris).

"The bump and run" was still very much the traditional shot for approaching the green as executed by Andrew Kirkaldy.

This illustration shows a typical "St Andrews Swing" based on the long-hitting (for that time), Hugh Kirkaldy. It was a full and energetic swipe—reminiscent of John Daly's 100 years later!

The last home-based Scot to win an Open at St Andrews—Hugh Kirkaldy.

Hugh Kirkaldy wearing his Championship Medal.

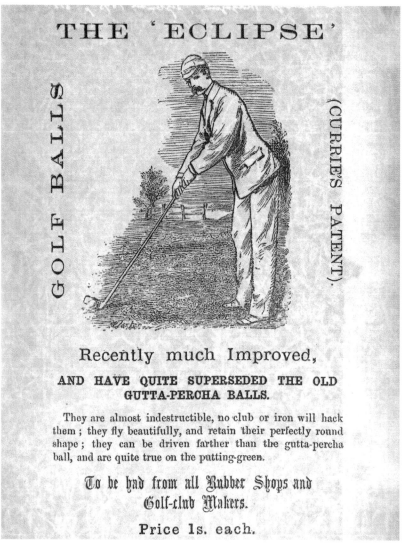

THE 'ECLIPSE'

GOLF BALLS

(CURRIE'S PATENT).

Recently much Improved,

AND HAVE QUITE SUPERSEDED THE OLD GUTTA-PERCHA BALLS.

They are almost indestructible, no club or iron will hack them; they fly beautifully, and retain their perfectly round shape; they can be driven farther than the gutta-percha ball, and are quite true on the putting-green.

To be had from all Rubber Shops and Golf-club Makers.

Price 1s. each.

The first magazine, *Golf* was published in 1890 and included an advert for the eclipse golf ball. Golf companies were springing up throughout the country and competition for the ball market was fierce, with varying gimmicks and patterns such as "the bramble"—weird and wonderful names for balls— "The Dot and Dash," "The White Imp," "The Colonel," "The Conqueror," "The Scottish King," and "The Auchterlonie Flier."

Above left: The wall behind the green and the station master's house are probably the only recognisable features today in this photograph of the Road Hole (the seventeenth). Note the disinterested caddie as he leans on and spikes the green with his golfer's umbrella! His colleague has one of the first golf bags tucked under his arm. The introduction of the canvas bag in the late 1880s sent shock waves through the St Andrews caddie ranks. Were they about to become an endangered species? The thought of their man, setting off with his "new-fangled carrier" down the first fairway without them caused many a bottom lip to quiver.

Left: A typical summer's day in the 1890s on the links with the start of play halfway down the first fairway.

Mr John Ball, the first English winner of the Open in 1890.

Mr S. Mure Fergusson, representing the R&A, was the leading amateur.

Local favourite Andrew Kirkaldy waits to putt as Willie Park Jr, watched by his caddie, "Fiery" (on the right), holes out on the first green. Large crowds followed this and similar challenge matches before and after the Championship itself, which was to be the last Open of two rounds played over the one day.

From Hamilton Hall, the last of the summer light throws shadow from the Valley of Sin across all the undulations of the eighteenth fairway.

1895-1910

EMERGENCE
OF THE
TRIUMVIRATE

1895

THE OPEN CAME BACK TO ST ANDREWS ON WEDNESDAY THE 12TH OF JUNE—A MUCH LESS HOSTILE TIME OF YEAR—AND AT LEAST THEY WOULDN'T RUN OUT OF LIGHT BEFORE THE END OF PLAY. BUT OTHER PROBLEMS EMERGED. THE OLD WOULD ALWAYS HAVE THE LAST SAY AS A LINKS COURSE IN THE RUNNING OF THINGS, AS WAS PROVEN IN THIS REPORT FROM THE *ST ANDREWS CITIZEN* ON THE CONDITION OF THE COURSE:

"Up till Wednesday the course was in a very arid condition. Everywhere the grass was burnt up with the sun, and the putting greens for the past week had been excessively keen and untrustworthy. After a dull and threatening afternoon on Tuesday Old Tom Morris, despairing of the promised rain, turned out his men with the hose and watered the greens. As luck would have it, however, their labour was scarcely finished when the heavens broke, and a short but very heavy downpour of rain fell, which followed afterwards by light intermittent showers, served materially to freshen and revivify the course."

So Old Tom got lucky with the weather! He even played the four rounds of the Championship—but probably wished he hadn't. With a first round of 107, he eventually finished 70 shots behind the winner, J.H. Taylor. In his defence it has to be said that he was 73 years old. He was the first to step onto the last green and shake hands with Taylor and congratulate him on his victory. Tom Morris may have lost his firm grip on his game, but he was certainly in full control of the course as Custodian of the Links. In fact, he seemed to be a law unto himself, as indicated in a letter to the Secretary by A.F. MacFie, the first Amateur Champion, and a member of the Royal and Ancient:

Dear Mr Grace,

I have thought the matter over, and I am afraid I must decline to serve on the green committee, as long as the green committee is a mere collective puppet in Tom Morris's hands. I think it is a perfect farce having one at all: and till a green committee would be supported by the general feeling of the Club in any dispute with Morris—which is far from being the case at present—there is no earthly use in trying to improve the course in any way.

Yours truly,
A.F. MacFie

It is interesting to note how commercial aspects of the game were influencing its image. In the first Opens the weather report seemed to have been featured more than the actual recording of the event. By 1895 St Andrews was described as, "The Mecca of Golf crowded with pilgrims drawn thither to witness the great contest." Adverts for balls, clubs, greenkeeping equipment, and even course design were in every newspaper. Although he was an amateur player, Harold Hilton could be seen on billboards advertising Woodbine cigarettes. (He was rarely seen without one hanging from his mouth when playing.) Willie Park Jr, son of the first winner and an Open champion himself in 1887 and 1889—although still on top of his game—did not play.

He said he had too many commitments to design courses.

The New Course opened that year because of the excessive amount of play on the Old Course. Tom Morris had a hand in its design, and the Royal and Ancient paid £1,763 for it—just under £100 a hole! The New Course—which was eventually to be used as a qualifying course for the Open—was considered more difficult than the Old Course at the time, "with frightening hazards." The day after the Open, the top 20 played a round in a competition on the New Course, and the scoring reflected this. Andrew Kirkaldy won, with a course record of 85.

The Tournament

Crowds followed Willie Fernie, Harry Vardon, Ben Sayers, Willie Auchterlonie, Sandy Herd, Hugh Kirkaldy, Andrew Kirkaldy, and defending champion J.H. Taylor on the first day, but the majority of spectators tended to roam the course at a varying pace, seeking out interesting players. Thirty-seven couples started play. At the end of the first day a second draw was introduced—not as the "cut," but to give a number of players, having done badly, the opportunity to retire and six withdrew! Looking at the draw, they were still teeing off at the traditional startup time of 10:00 am at five-minute intervals. J.H. Taylor started the first of his last two rounds just before noon. The Open that year built up to an exciting finish, with the last players on the course all in contention. This was purely coincidental with the way the second day draw was pulled from the hat.

When you look at Herd, Taylor, and Kirkaldy's cards for the four rounds there were a lot of sixes scattered about them but only two sevens—belonging to Sandy Herd—both at the 5th. The 8th hole seemed the easiest on the course—recording twelve par 3s—while on the short 11th they could manage only four pars between them, adding five bogies, two double bogies, and a six! The 14th proved most difficult, producing only three pars. The 16th was a key hole, with Taylor managing three pars and a bogie, while Herd and Kirkaldy struggled with seven bogies and two double bogies.

Taylor won the admiration of everyone on the last round when he battled against the two locals, Herd and Kirkaldy, in driving wind and rain. At one point he trailed Herd by five shots, but with typical grit and determination, not only did he master the conditions but he shot 78 for the second time in the Championship, while more than half the field could not break 90.

J.H. Taylor

John Henry Taylor was born near the Devon Links of Westward Ho in the West Country of England in 1871. He became a caddie at an early age and often listened to stories of the three Allan brothers, who were the professionals at the Royal North Devon Club at that time. He was in awe of the great matches they had played in, and in particular of Jamie Allan, who had made the long trip up to St Andrews and was runner-up to Anderson there in the 1879 Open.

By 18 years of age, Taylor was appointed the professional at Burnham in Somerset and was put up against Andrew Kirkaldy, who had just lost in a play-off to Willie Park Jr in the Open at Musselburgh that year (1889). Kirkaldy had come down to be the pro at Winchester. The match was two rounds at Burnham and two at the Winchester course, which Taylor won. So impressed were the Winchester supporters that they eventually persuaded the young Taylor to change allegiance in 1892 and represent them.

His record in the Open was formidable—winning at Sandwich in 1894 and the following year at St Andrews. He barely failed to add a third consecutive title by losing in a play-off at Muirfield to Harry Vardon. He was runner-up on no less than six occasions, and but for the rub of the green could have beaten Vardon's all-time record of six Open wins.

After his second win at St Andrews he went out to the States and was again runner-up to Vardon in the U.S. Open. The game was becoming international, and he picked up the new French Open title in 1908 and 1909, as well as another Open Championship at Deal that year. His fifth Open win—in 1913 at Hoylake—was by an eight-shot margin, as it had also been in St Andrews in 1900.

Taylor had moved from Winchester to Richmond and finally to Royal Mid-Surrey, where he was resident for 47 years. He was such an asset to the game and instrumental in setting up the Professional Golfers Association, of which he was the main ambassador. It was through his image and his eloquence that the profile of the professional golfer was raised to a new and respectable level. Things were about to change in comparison with the old times when "a gloved gentleman" could be heard justifying his defeat by a professional by saying, "Why of course the chap beat me—he does nothing but play golf."

After the war, at age 51, J.H. Taylor was only one shot off the lead going into the last round of the Open at Sandwich in 1922. He went on to captain the Ryder Cup in 1933, and was made an Honorary Member of the Royal and Ancient in 1950 and president of the Royal North Devon Club in 1957. He died in 1963 at the ripe old age of 91.

The Triumvirate

After the original "Big Three" of Morris, Robertson, and

Park, emerged another group just as formidable four decades later. The "Triumvirate" of Harry Vardon, J.H. Taylor, and James Braid dominated the game from 1895 to 1914, winning 16 Opens between them.

It is quite disappointing—almost unnatural—that Harry Vardon, like the Morrises, did not win an Open Championship at St Andrews. His record six wins were at Muirfield in 1896, three at Prestwick in 1898, 1903, and 1914, and at Sandwich in 1899 and 1911. As one of the greatest players of all time, he will be remembered for his elegant, upright swing and his flying right elbow. He was a greenkeeper's delight—hardly ever taking a divot, so sweet did he strike the ball. He was an innovator. The "Vardon Grip" took over from the hammer (split-handed) grip and the "swipe" of old became a swing, as brute force and ignorance were replaced by timing and control. The six or seven assorted clubs tucked under the arm were to become a matched set under his influence.

Born in Jersey in the Channel Islands in 1870, he came over to England after his older brother, Tom, had told him it was possible to make a living out of the game of golf. The two brothers were winner and runner-up in the 1903 Open, although Harry finished a comfortable six shots in front of his brother. Harry developed tuberculosis, which, unlike two former champions, wasn't to kill him at an early age, but plagued him throughout his distinguished career.

Freddie Tait, the great Amateur Champion, about to complete his round with Tom Morris, at the edge of the green, seemingly lining up the putt for him!

PRICE-LIST.

ALL GOODS HAND MADE.

	EACH.		EACH.
Drivers,	5/	Balls, ...	6d. and 8d.
Long Spoons,	5/	Morris' Agrippa,	1/
Mid Spoons,	5/	Morris' Machine-Made Balls,	1/3
Short Spoons,	5/	Morris' Special Balls,	1/9
Putters,	5/	Hickory. Headed Drivers,	6/
Brassys,	6/	„ „ Bulgers,	6/6
Irons,	5/6	„ „ Brassys,	7/6
Cleeks,	5/6	Dogwood Headed Drivers,	5/
Iron Niblicks,	5/6	„ „ Bulgers,	5/
Mashies,	5/6	„ „ Brassys,	6/
Iron Putters,	5/6	Persimmon Headed Drivers,	5/
Morris' Patent Cleek,	7/6	„ „ Bulgers,	5/
Bulgers,	5/	„ „ Brassys,	6/
Broad-headed Bulgers,	5/6	Special Iron Putter,	6/6
Morris' Patent Niblick,	7/6	„ Mashie,	6/6
Bulger Heads,	3/	„ Cleeks,	6/6
Broad-headed Bulger Heads,	3/6	Gun Metal Putters,	6/
Driver, Putter, Long, Mid, and		Ladies' Drivers,	5/
Short Spoon Heads,	3/	„ Bulgers,	5/
Brassy Heads,	3/6	„ Brassys,	6/
Cleek, Iron, and Niblick Heads,	3/6	„ Putters,	5/
Morris' Patent Cleek Heads,	5/6	All Ladies' Iron Clubs,	5/6
Morris' Patent Niblick Heads,	5/6	Boys' Clubs, from	3/6
Shafts,	2/	„ Cleeks and Irons, from	3/6
Special Do., 6d. extra.		„ Toy Clubs,	1/6
BALLS RE-MADE, 4s. PER DOZEN.		BALLS RE-MADE, 4s. PER DOZEN.	

ALL GOODS HAND MADE.

SPECIALTIES.

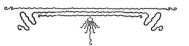

	EACH.
The New Socket Clubs,	6/
The New Socket Brassys,	7/
The "Tom Morris" Long Faced Bulgers,	5/
The "Tom Morris" Long Faced Brassys,	6/
The "Tom Morris" Long Faced Socket Bulgers,	6/
The "Tom Morris" Long Faced Socket Brassys,	7/

DAVID WATT, TYPO., DUNFERMLINE.

TOM MORRIS,
Wholesale & Retail Golf Club Manufacturer,
ST. ANDREWS.

REPAIRS EXECUTED BY EXPERIENCED WORKMEN.

**GOLF COVERS AND ALL REQUISITES
FOR THE GAME OF GOLF.** . . . . .

Morris' Machine-Made Balls.

This Tom Morris price list—current during the 1895 Open—shows how "Brassys" and "Bulgers" (the new, shorter, wooden-headed clubs) were replacing the long-nose spoons and playclubs (drivers) of what was a bygone era. Although the shop featured long-faced clubs in its brochure as "Specialities," their days were numbered.

Tourism in the Victorian era was booming in St Andrews. During the summer months weekly reports were published in the *St Andrews Citizen* announcing who was visiting the town and where they were staying—probably as a deterrent to anyone planning an illicit weekend away from home!

It was a tradition that Tom Morris should act as starter for all the R&A Spring and Autumn Meetings and challenge matches and tend the pin on the last hole for selected matches. Even when at home he would keep an eye on the last green from the top window above his shop. If anyone was seen loitering or, heaven forbid, took a practise swing on it, they would soon be reprimanded from above!

Far left: Mr Harold Hilton was one of the great Amateur Champions winning in 1900 and 1901, as well as being the first Open Champion at Muirfield in 1892 and the first winner at Hoylake in 1897. Along with Mr John Ball—the first Englishman to win the Open in 1890—they both represented Royal Liverpool.

Left: Freddie Tait, a Lieutenant in the Black Watch, was killed in action during the Boer War in 1900. Having won the Amateur in 1896 and 1898, he was prominent in the Open Championship during this period until his untimely death at the age of 30. This photograph shows him (centre) preparing to tee off for the last time on the Old Course in September 1899.

Below: Tom Morris became a legend in his own time and was the most photographed and written-about golfer. His picture appeared in a variety of publications—books, magazines, and postcards—and his comments on the game were much sought after. With his competitive playing days over, "The Grand Old Man of Golf" travelled the country from Shetland to Ireland designing a variety of golf courses or "laying out a green." His fee was one pound a day plus expenses. He adapted Carnoustie in 1867 and laid out the original Muirfield course in 1891—Royal County Down and Rosapenna in Ireland—Royal Dornoch, Tain, and Cruden Bay in the north of Scotland—Ladybank, Elie (now qualifying courses for the Open) and the New Course in St Andrews. He made many trips to England setting up courses such as Newcastle, Cleveland, Wallasey, and Hanger Hill near London. It seemed his "catchphrase" for opening most courses he had designed was, "This is most probably the finest course in the land!"

The R&A Clubhouse has gone though many structural changes since its original design and construction in 1854. Through the years as the game expanded, so too did the building. This 1895 photograph of Old Tom Morris and group shows the club before the second floor and the now familiar Secretary's balcony were added in 1899.

Hugh Philp, the master clubmaker of the town, died in 1856. His nephew, Robert Forgan, took over the business. As the game grew, "Forgan's" became the world's first, and biggest, golf club manufacturer by the 1880s, but struggled after the transition from hickory to steel shafts in the late 1920s and is sadly no more.

Having started his career as a feather golf ball maker in the 1840s—making two a day—Tom Morris finished his career selling dozens of gutty balls throughout the country by advertising his wares.

This illustration features the winner of the 1895 Open, J.H. Taylor, with all the main contenders grouped behind him.

1900

BACK CAME TAYLOR IN 1900 TO DEFEND HIS ST ANDREWS WIN OF 1895. HARRY VARDON WAS "THE MAIN MAN," HAVING WON THREE OF THE LAST FOUR OPENS. VARDON—WHO HAD JUST RETURNED FROM THE STATES AFTER A GRUELLING 20,000-MILE TOUR, PLAYING AND PROMOTING THE GAME—LOOKED SHARP DESPITE SUCH A PUNISHING TRIP. HE WOULD MAKE TWO OTHER EXHAUSTING AMERICAN TOURS IN 1913 AND 1920.

Taylor and Vardon both scored 79 in the opening round—the only two to break 80. Taylor gained four shots on the second round, with a record-equalling 77 for the Old Course in tournament play. (Sandy Herd had achieved it in the 1895 Open and Young Tom Morris over 25 years before, but not in tournament play.) It was an indication—considering such improvements in equipment and in the course itself—of just how good Young Tom must have been in his day.

J.H. Taylor was majestic, and strode away from the field with yet another score under 80. In the final round a tremendous crowd—the biggest ever recorded—followed Taylor. He rose to the occasion and, apart from being bunkered off the tee at the sixth, was in complete control, finishing with a new championship record of 75, beating Vardon by eight shots. James Braid was third, 13 strokes behind.

The following is a quote from *The Scotsman*:

"There will be no disposition in any quarter to grudge J.H. Taylor the victory he won at St Andrews. It was a victory due to superb golf in every department of the game. In the hands of Vardon and Taylor it would almost appear that golf is losing its 'glorious uncertainty' which many regard as its peculiar attraction."

Old Tom "posing" again on the first tee for the camera.

Sandy Herd, a St Andrean and winner of the 1902 Open at Hoylake, paired with James Braid, represented Scotland in many challenge matches against Vardon and Taylor, playing for England. Those matches toured around the country, attracting big crowds. Herd is seen in this photograph driving off the first tee prior to the 1900 Open at St Andrews.

Caddie Davy Corstorphine awaits instruction from his Caddie Master, pipe-smoking James Jolly.

The town built its own railway to join up with the North British line three miles away, and even bought its own train! In the 1850s, the accessibility of courses through the railway network and the availability of the new ball created a sudden surge of interest in the game. Noisy old steam trains, billowing smoke as they skirted the edge of the fifteenth and sixteenth holes, were a dramatic feature of the homeward stretch on the Old Course. The railway, despite its dominance, was axed in 1969. There is still an ongoing campaign to bring it back to St Andrews.

The first car in St Andrews after the 1900 Open caused quite a stir. It was an Argyle, bought by George Rusack, son of the founder of Rusack's Hotel. It was driven onto the Old Course for the townsfolk to see. Tom Morris was photographed perched on the driving seat with his granddaughter who had married George. The Argyle was one of only 16 built in Scotland in 1902.

J.H. Taylor, with his distinctive flat-footed stance, hits to the green, and is robbed as the ball lips round the hole and another birdie chance slips by.

Testing the town's fire engine on an occasional Sunday afternoon always seemed to attract great attention as many people took their traditional walk out and around the Old Course. The Old was always closed on the Sabbath and remains so today, with the recent exception of the Open Championship or any other major tournament hosted by the town. As Old Tom was heard to say, "The course needs a rest even if you don't, sir."

The Triumvirate of Vardon, Taylor, and Braid dominated the Open from 1894 to the outbreak of the First World War. Between them they won 16 Championships during this period. Braid and Taylor both won five times and both won twice at St Andrews. Although Vardon never won here, he still holds the record of most wins in the Championship, having held the Claret Jug aloft on six occasions.

1905

BORN IN ELIE IN 1870, 12 MILES FROM ST ANDREWS, JAMES BRAID WON FIVE OPEN CHAMPIONSHIPS FROM 1901 TO 1910, AND WAS RUNNER-UP ON THREE OCCASIONS. HE WAS A DOUBLE WINNER AT ST ANDREWS IN 1905 AND 1910 AND AT MUIRFIELD IN 1901 AND 1906.

A tall man, he hit the ball long distances and was the first player to break 70 in an Open at Sandwich in 1904. He was active in golf all of his life, up to his 80th year in 1950. Not only was he a great champion at the turn of the century, but he was also renowned as a golf course designer, his most famous courses being the Kings and Queens at Gleneagles and the reconstruction of Carnoustie prior to its first Open Championship in 1931. He was responsible for designing 39 major courses in Britain.

During his first win at St Andrews, his boyhood hero, the 1879 winner, Jamie Anderson, died. *Golf Illustrated* wrote at the time, "Thus the Open Champion who has gone may have been, in a sense the making of the Open Champion who bears the distinction today." As a nine-year-old, Braid followed Anderson around the links of Elie until the former champion took notice of him. After seeing the young boy swing and hit a couple of shots for him, Jamie earnestly told the boy that if he kept practising and playing, one day he too could become the Open champion.

Inspired by this, James Braid became a scratch golfer at the age of 16. He moved to St Andrews as an apprentice carpenter and then to London as a clubmaker. He became the professional at Walton Heath, a major club in England, and held that position for 46 years.

James Braid—a quiet and considerate man—was without doubt one of the most respected characters in golf, as shown in this acknowledgment to the editor of *Golf Illustrated*:

Sir—

Will you kindly allow me a small space in your valuable paper to express my sincere thanks to all those friends and golfers who have so kindly sent telegrams and letters of congratulation on my winning the championship, as they are much too numerous for me to answer personally. Thanking you in anticipation,

I am, Sir, etc.,
Jas. Braid
Walton Heath Golf Club, June 16th, 1905

He wrote an illustrated book called *Advanced Golf* in 1906, which was reprinted eight times in four years, such was his popularity. All professional golfers took note of his teaching methods and opinions on how the game should be played. As well as being able to slice or hook the ball at will, he was an outstanding putter, using a heavy aluminium-headed weapon with a short backswing.

Along with J.H. Taylor and Willie Auchterlonie, he was made an Honorary Member of the Royal and Ancient Golf Club in 1950—many years after Tom Morris had become the first.

1905

After Tom Morris had at last retired there was much criticism of the course. With the Haskell, a new rubber-cored "bounding ball," now in use, it was feared by the new greenkeeper, Hugh Hamilton, and the committee that the

Old Course might be vulnerable to the crack professionals. Surely Taylor's course record would go. Calculations and prophecies of great scores were not to come true, partly because they had lengthened certain tees and created even more pot bunkers around the course. Many of the players criticised the pots' severity and the lack of room to get in and out of them—never mind about swinging a club! Some of the competitors, in their disgust, had irreverently called the new bunkers "spittoons." Despite yet another record number of entries, only a dozen scores under 80 were recorded. The lowest score was a 77 from Rowland Jones in the second round. In fairness to the players, strong crosswinds on the first day's play did make it difficult to score well.

James Braid, although having won at Muirfield in 1901,

had been runner-up on three other occasions. It was Taylor's turn to be second yet again, five shots behind. With a gallery of 4,000 following Braid, he seemed to be coasting until he was forced to play off the railway line on the 15th. He was in trouble yet again on the 16th, having hit a "spittoon," which was a new antisocial addition to the middle of the fairway. Having already dug one out of the "Principal's Nose" after being bunkered off the tee, he thrashed the next onto the railway line again and found himself up against a sleeper. He had trouble moving the ball at all, but eventually it shot through the green—and a miraculous pitch back to six inches saved the hole.

For all the talk of the revolutionary new ball changing the game, Braid's comfortable win was, in fact, nine shots behind Taylor's score with the gutty ball in 1900.

Group of past Open winners congregating around the R&A steps to the first tee. Left to right: J.H. Taylor, Jack White, Mr Harold Hilton, Mr John Ball, James Braid, Tom Morris, Bob Ferguson, Willie Auchterlonie, Jamie Anderson, Hugh Kirkaldy, Bob Martin, and Willie Fernie. Seated on the grass from left to right: Sandy Herd, Harry Vardon, Willie Park Jr, and Jack Simpson.

In the final round at the sixteenth, Braid was bunkered off the tee and hit from sand onto the railway line—not out-of-bounds at that time, but against a sleeper on the track. He failed to move the ball on his first attempt then thinned it to the back of the green. A wonderfully delicate chip back saved the hole and Braid went on to win by five shots.

Spectators rush across the Swilken Bridge to witness Braid's triumphant walk down the 18th fairway.

James Braid, with rounds of 81, 78, 78, and 81, holes out on the last green to win the 1905 Open.

Cartoon from *Golf Illustrated* shows the leading players of the day, who had complained bitterly about the addition of new pot bunkers. Liberally scattered about the course, they referred to them as "spittoons!"

Adverts crammed the pages of *Golf Illustrated*–from wonder belts to balls!

Right: "Putting Green Manure"

Hugh Hamilton, a greenkeeper at Portrush in Ireland, took over as the Keeper of the Green after Tom Morris had retired in 1902. He advertised his putting green manure in 1905 in one of the April issues of *Golf Illustrated*–"The Weekly Organ of The Royal and Ancient Game." Either he was sold out immediately or had so little response that it was never advertised again!

Tom Morris died on 24th May 1908 after a bad fall down the wine cellar steps of the New Club, aged 86. The whole town closed down, including the golf courses—even the schools—for the funeral which progressed through the streets to the cathedral where "The Grand Old Man" was finally laid to rest by the side of Young Tom's grave, some 33 years after the untimely death of his son.

Tom Morris's portrait which hangs in the Royal and Ancient Clubhouse is a fine oil painting by Sir George Reid, a club member and eminent artist. Old Tom was taken to Sir George's studio in Edinburgh and told that, because the portrait may take a while, he was to adopt a position appertaining to golf in which he felt comfortable. Striking this now familiar pose, Old Tom was asked what it signified. He replied, "I am just waiting for the gentlemen to play." On seeing the portrait unveiled, he was asked for his opinion of it, of which he said, "...The bunnet's like mine."

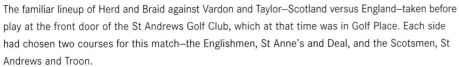

The familiar lineup of Herd and Braid against Vardon and Taylor—Scotland versus England—taken before play at the front door of the St Andrews Golf Club, which at that time was in Golf Place. Each side had chosen two courses for this match—the Englishmen, St Anne's and Deal, and the Scotsmen, St Andrews and Troon.

James Braid was a powerful hitter of the ball but, although his swing looked ungainly at times (it often seemed as if he was chasing after the ball on his follow-through), he had great control in fading or drawing the ball at will.

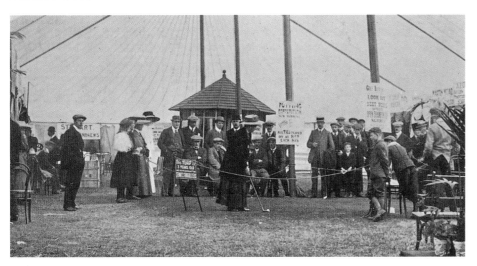

Left: Trying out the new Braid Mills heavy-headed putters in the first exhibition tent at a St Andrews Open.

1910

A 260-FOOT-LONG TENT, 60 FEET WIDE, WAS ERECTED ON THE BRUCE EMBANKMENT FOR THE FIFTIETH ANNIVERSARY OPEN IN 1910. IT WAS THE LARGEST EVER ERECTED IN SCOTLAND AT THAT TIME.

The embankment was named after George Bruce, a St Andrews Provost, who around the time of the first Open here in 1873—out of his own pocket—paid for some old and derelict galleons to be towed in from around the coast and hauled into position to create a breakwater. In this area (to the side of the first green) they were packed with the town's refuse, filled in, and turfed. This newly reclaimed land effectively stopped a high tide from encroaching on, or eroding, the course.

The Exhibition

"A competitive exhibition!" was how this new innovation was advertised. Inside the huge tent were 60 stalls. The competitive side of it was to award gold medals for best drivers, brassies, and wooden putters. Auchterlonie of St Andrews had picked up three gold medals and a diploma at Deal the previous year and promoted a display involving the 47 stages in the making of a custom-built driver (as compared to the three stages involved in assembling a club today!).

There were seven main St Andrews club manufacturers showing their wares, famous names at the time, such as Forgan's, attracting much attention. Tom Morris's stall featured Young Tom's championship medal of 1872.

Scotland vs England

The exhibition was set up for the weekend before the Open as "The Big Match"—Scotland vs England was on Saturday and pulled in big crowds. The Triumvirate had been up practising prior to this, along with all the top names. England beat Scotland by eight games to two, with Vardon beating Braid in the first game. The afternoon foursomes were drawn three apiece. Braid got revenge when paired with Sandy Herd, when they beat Vardon and Taylor by five and four.

The Championship

There was much speculation as to which of the Triumvirate might emerge victorious. All three entered with four Open Championship wins to their name. There were 210 competitors—199 professionals and 11 amateurs—who all had aspirations of doing well, but the delegates decided that only the top 60 scores would go through to the second day's rounds.

The couple who played off first at 8:30 on Tuesday morning had signed and handed in their cards by 10:40! They must have scurried round the course to avoid the dark storm clouds, which were looming ominously on the

James Braid's (right) triumph at winning at St Andrews in 1910 had an extra edge to it, for he held the record for five wins in the Open, but it was short-lived, for Harry Vardon (left) came back at him the next year, then claimed a sixth win in 1914 at Prestwick.

horizon. When James Braid set out on his round about lunchtime, a thunderstorm had developed and surrounded the course. The greens were saturated within an hour and balls were floating around the pins on the opening holes. The committee eventually decided to cancel the day's play and all the recorded scores. Braid had a 76—an amazing round in such conditions. When he was told to come off the course after battling to the 13th, he decided to play the round out just in case he had been misinformed.

Two rounds were crammed into the next day. Willie Smith, who in the 1905 Open represented Nassau, USA, rocketed into the lead with a 77 in the afternoon and a record-equalling 71 in the evening. Smith had emigrated from Carnoustie and won the American Open in 1899. He was the first official United States entrant in the Championship to play at St Andrews.

Only those returning the 60 lowest scores took part in the final two rounds. A Scot, George Duncan—the quickest player ever seen (he wrote a book called *Golf at the Gallop*)— with a 73, 77, and 71, was ahead of Braid and Herd going into the last round, but the pressure got to him. Bernard

Darwin wrote of Duncan's demise: "From the first tee he showed signs very palpable of natural anxiety...he was constantly weak and short in his approaching and early on got fours by the skin of his teeth by holing difficult putts... sixes at both the 5th and 6th were disastrous and although he steadied for a while, one calamity succeeded another and his golf may be fairly called demoralised." George Duncan, despite this setback, went on to win in 1920 in a fearless finish after being 13 shots behind at the halfway point.

Braid—the record holder for most championships won— was carried aloft after his second win at St Andrews, but not for long, for his partners in the Triumvirate soon caught up. Vardon had the last say after he took his sixth title at Prestwick in 1914 just before the Great War.

Apart from Braid and Taylor, only Peter Thomson and Tom Watson have come close to emulating Vardon's feat in recent times.

Below: Competition between The Triumvirate was even keener in 1910 as it was the fiftieth anniversary of the Open and a Jubilee Medal, as well as a commemorative print featuring the winner, were produced that year.

Far left: The Jubilee Medal.

Left: George Duncan at the sixteenth hole.

Below left: The old portable bathing hut had gone and had been replaced by a more stable starter's box.

Below: James Braid, putting on the last green in 1910, was to be the last action in a St Andrews Open until 1921.

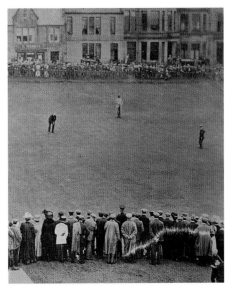

James Braid in national dress.

Right: There could not have been a more popular winner in St Andrews at the time than local man, James Braid.

A brooding storm cloud hangs over the Swilken Bridge as daisies submerge by an R&A reflection in "casual water after the heavens opened!"

1921~1933

THE AMERICAN INVASION

1921

THE FIRST AMERICAN TO WIN THE OPEN CHAMPIONSHIP WAS FROM ST ANDREWS!

AN ODD STATEMENT, SURELY, BUT IN FACT THE WINNER OF THE 1921 OPEN WAS JOCK

HUTCHISON, BORN AND BRED IN THE TOWN. HE HAD EMIGRATED JUST BEFORE THE WAR

AND BECAME AN AMERICAN CITIZEN.

This was an Open full of incident. Even the local golf columnist James Sorlay, Secretary of the St Andrews Golf Club, got a bit carried away in reporting the week's proceedings. "There was never an Open Championship like this one, thousands and thousands were privileged to witness it. There may never be another like it. In every sense of the word it was a record championship—record crowds (despite the coal strike), record scores, wonderful weather and a championship meeting which from start to finish furnished such surprises and thrills that no previous meeting ever approached."

The Royal and Ancient had assumed sole responsibility for running the Open and had set two qualifying rounds on the Eden and the Old to narrow the field of 160 entrants down to 85. The 1912 Champion, Englishman Ted Ray—who had won the U.S. Open in 1920—just squeezed into the draw. The lineup included 12 Americans, one Spaniard, three Australians, three Frenchmen, and 56 British competitors.

Jock Hutchison was the favourite, having led the qualifying with Harry Vardon one shot behind. Hutchison, partnered with a young Bobby Jones, not only maintained his form but created a sensation in the first round when he holed-in-one at the 8th and then nearly did it again at the par-4 9th. Back-to-back eagles had taken him out in 33.

His only hiccup in the tournament was to have "a bad day on the greens" in the third round.

Walter Hagen attracted much attention during the week through his fashionable American attire, which complemented his style of play. He was to win four of the Opens during this decade.

Roger Wethered, an amateur representing the Royal and Ancient, had a great championship, and was leading on the final day despite having stepped on his ball in the third round at the 5th hole, incurring a penalty.

There was criticism over Jock Hutchison using a "ribbed iron," which was said gave him an unfair advantage in spinning the ball back sharply onto such hard and inhospitable greens. J.H. Taylor described it as "buying the shot out of a shop."

The outcome of the four rounds of play was announced as a tie—Jock Hutchison and Roger Wethered at 296, Tom Kerrigan (USA) at 298, Arthur Havers (who would win at Troon in 1923) at 299, and George Duncan (the previous year's winner) at 301. And so it was to be a two-round playoff—a head-to-head—the gentleman against the professional. Hutchison won comfortably, taking an unassailable lead, turning in 33 in the first round. On the second round he took 43 to come home, but still won by a margin of 9 shots.

There was controversy on the last green as the final putt was holed, as reported by *The St Andrews Citizen*:

"Mr Wethered played like a sportsman and heartily congratulated the winner at the finish of the game but his fellow member, the Chairman of the R&A Championship Committee was such a poor loser that he practically threw the cup at the new champion—immediately he called for three cheers for Roger Wethered. With no speech-making or presentation the crowd dispersed for there was nothing more for them to see."

This unfortunate scene left an unpleasant impression, and made many—there to see the climax of an exciting week—indignant. Jock Hutchison was upset, and it took the edge off his delight in taking the Claret Jug across the Atlantic for the first time in its history.

The Rules Committee had met the month before and had declared "ribbed irons" such as Hutchison's illegal, but this was not implemented until a week after the Open. Also, the Old Course took a battering. A notice went up one week later:

"Because of excessive tear and wear occasioned by the Open Championship and the drought it will be temporarily closed 'til further notice."

This was an extreme decision at the height of a short summer season.

Jock Hutchison playing a short approach with his controversial ribbed iron.

Jock outside the St Andrews Golf Club (his orig-inal home club) with a driver, brassie, and four wood.

Right: Jock Hucthison meets up with Max Faulkner (winner at Portrush in 1951) and Ken Bousfield at the start of the Centenary Open in 1960, nearly 40 years after his win at St Andrews.

Alister Mackenzie's famous drawing of the Old Course, which hangs in the R&A Secretary's office.

Despite the suspension of championship golf in Scotland due to the Great War, big crowds welcomed the Open back to St Andrews in 1921 to witness yet more drama and trauma in the evolution and continuing popularity of the tournament.

A valiant attempt to stop the green at the sixteenth from becoming water-logged during play—but you wouldn't fancy the next putt on it!

1927

MR ROBERT TYRE "BOBBY" JONES ARRIVED BACK IN ST ANDREWS IN A BLAZE OF GLORY, HAVING WON THE AMERICAN OPEN FOR THE SECOND TIME AND THE CHAMPIONSHIP THE YEAR BEFORE AT LYTHAM. IN ALL THE LOCAL COLUMNS WRITTEN ABOUT THE 1921 OPEN, "THE BOY WONDER'S" ONLY MENTION WAS, "MR ROBERT JONES JNR RETIRED IN THE THIRD ROUND." HE HAD IN FACT BEEN LEADING ALL THE AMATEURS, INCLUDING ROGER WETHERED, AFTER TWO ROUNDS, BUT ON DAY THREE HE STRUGGLED IN A TYPICAL OLD COURSE CROSSWIND AND WENT OUT IN 46. HE DOUBLE-BOGEYED THE 10TH, THEN WITH FOUR STABS AT THE BALL TO GET OUT OF THE DEEP "HILL" BUNKER AT THE SHORT 11TH, HE TORE UP HIS CARD.

It was a different story on his return to challenge the Old Course six years later. He opened up with a record-breaking 68 in the first round, holing everything. Apart from bunkering himself off the second tee in three of his four rounds, he was in complete control of the situation. Further rounds of 72, 73, and 72 saw him win by six shots in a new Championship record of 285.

Such was the impact of the charismatic Jones that at one time the great Harry Vardon had to stand behind his own ball to protect it as crowds charged past him to see the younger man play!

The great golf writer Bernard Darwin described the scene after Bobby Jones modestly claimed his victory:

"As soon as the last putt was holed the greater part of the multitude (about 15,000 in the area) surged up the slope— and enveloped the champion. Even Captain Lindbergh in Paris or at Croydon cannot have been in more imminent fear of asphyxiation than was the champion for one or two anxious moments. Then clasping his famous "Calamity Jane" tightly in his hand he was hoisted upon willing shoulders while hundreds of hands patted him on the back or any other available portion of him. The crowd swung this way and that with its burden. Bobby's cap was soon irretrievably lost, but still he held his putter inviolate over his head. At long last he was safely on the ground again and the admiring crowd followed him, gazing and patting until he was safe in his hotel."

Many things have been written and said about Jones, the man, and his career, in particular of his "Grand Slam" in 1930...winning the British and U.S. Open and Amateur Championships in the same year. In particular, Sidney Matthew's book, *The Life and Times of Bobby Jones*, is a fitting tribute.

As a St Andrean I have tried not to be biased or parochial about our local heroes in reporting past Championships, but I have to say that Bobby Jones has a special place in our

ROYAL BURGH OF ST. ANDREWS

Freedom of the Burgh

TO

MR. ROBERT T. JONES, Jr.

OF ATLANTA, GEORGIA, U.S.A.

IN THE

Younger Graduation Hall, St. Andrews,

ON

Thursday, 9th October 1958, at 8.30 p.m.

This ticket will admit one person to the Back Area

Seats must be occupied by 8.20 p.m.

In red ermine-lined robe, the St Andrews Provost congratulates Bobby Jones after handing over a silver casket and conferring "The Freedom of the City" on him in 1958. The cherished ticket is mine, as my father and I attended when I was nine years old.

An excited crowd mobbed a triumphant Bobby Jones as he was carried aloft.

Hill bunker, to the side of the 11th green, shows the steepness of its face where Jones came to a miserable end in the third round of the 1921 Open.

hearts. More significant to us in the town was "The St Andrews Grand Slam" he had achieved by 1958. At an emotional presentation ceremony in a packed Younger Hall, he was made an Honorary Burgess and granted the Freedom of the City, to add to his other three honorary memberships of the Royal and Ancient, St Andrews, and New Golf Clubs. As a nine-year-old boy, I stood with my father as all the guests rose at the end of the ceremony and spontaneously burst into singing, "Will Ye No' Come Back Again." It still seems to echo around that hall. My father, as a nine-year-old boy, had in turn stood with his father, and watched Bobby Jones win the Amateur Championship on the Old Course in the first leg of "The Grand Slam."

Jones, on that memorable day the 9th October 1958, in his acceptance speech said of the Old Course: "The more I studied the course, the more I loved it...the more I loved it, the more I studied it."

His closing remark was: "If I could take out of my life everything but my experiences in St Andrews I would still have had a rich, full life."

After his death in 1971, at the following Spring R&A Meeting, a service of Thanksgiving and Commemoration for Robert Tyre Jones was given in the Town Church. Roger Wethered, who had fared so well in the 1921 Open, gave the main address to "A golfer matchless in skill and chivalrous in spirit." I was there with my father and as many townsfolk as the church could hold.

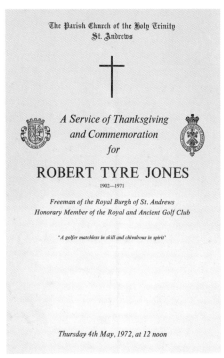

The cover of the Order of Ceremony printed for Jones's memorial service in 1972.

The parchment scroll handed over to Jones to commemorate his being made an Honorary Burgess—the first American to have received such an honour since Benjamin Franklin, a graduate of the University of St Andrews, some 200 years before.

Prior to the 1927 Open, the "Scoreboard" was simply a single sheet of paper posted on a board announcing the order of play. Eventually, the winner and the scores of everyone who had been in contention were displayed after the result was announced.

Jones received the Claret Jug after winning comfortably by six shots with scores of 68, 72, 73, and 72, setting a new Championship record.

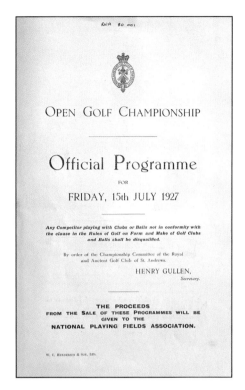

Jones starts the defence of his championship with a fine drive off the first tee, looking relaxed and in complete control of his swing, despite the pressure and hype that surrounded him.

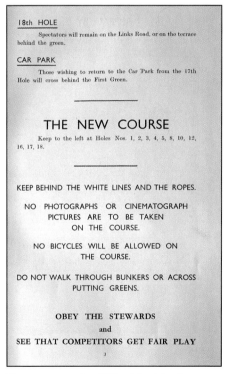

The programme for 1927—with advice for spectators watching qualifying on the New Course.

1933

THE RYDER CUP SQUADS OF AMERICA AND GREAT BRITAIN ALL PLAYED IN THIS ST ANDREWS OPEN. BRITAIN HAD WON THE CUP BY THE NARROWEST OF MARGINS, WITH DENSMORE SHUTE THREE-PUTTING IN THE LAST MATCH ON THE LAST GREEN AGAINST SYD EASTERBROOK. THERE WERE MANY FANCIED PLAYERS TEEING OFF IN THE CHAMPIONSHIP THAT YEAR BUT THEY WERE ALL TO FALL AWAY, QUITE DRAMATICALLY, IN THE LAST ROUND.

The course was playing "short but tricky." Parched brown fairways caused the ball to run on and on. For example, Craig Wood, the big, American hitter, caught the bunker on the ridge protecting the approach to the 5th green of the tee—a drive of 430 yards!

Sandy Herd, aged 65, qualified easily—in fact, ahead of the eventual winner. He'd played through many changes since he had first entered the Open in 1891 and won in 1902.

After the first round Hagen led the American challenge with a swashbuckling 68. His colleagues, Sarazen (the 1932 winner), Dudley, and Dunlap, were all in the hunt. The whole of the American Ryder Cup team went up to the Cathedral grounds that night and paid their respects to the Morrises, with Hagen laying a wreath at their graveside.

Walter Hagen, the four-time champion, maintained his lead comfortably at the halfway stage, but then played miserably—by his standards—with rounds of 79 and 82. It was a strange affair when, on the final round, Easterbrook, Mitchell, Cotton, Diegel, and Kirkwood were all vying for the lead, with Sarazen two shots behind, and Craig Wood,

with a 68 third round, was back in contention.

Densmore Shute from Cleveland, Ohio came in almost unnoticed with his fourth par 73 round in a row.

Sarazen got trapped in "Hell" at the 14th, and Cotton and Mitchell faded badly, both carding 79. Leo Diegel from the States looked set, but as Bernard Darwin reported on the final hole, Diegel was stone dead for his par, but somehow missed the putt "by the widest possible margin." He had fresh aired it and lost out by a shot!

Craig Wood, despite a 75 last round, tied with Densmore Shute for the championship at 292 (10 shots more than had been predicted). The two Americans prepared for a two-round play-off, but it had none of the drama and unpredictability of the previous day's play. Shute had started with two fours to Wood's two sixes and maintained that lead throughout the day.

Densmore Shute had been the most consistent player that week, but never broke par in qualifying, in the Championship, or in the playoff, but was still the new Open Champion of 1933!

Andrew Kirkaldy, Honorary Professional to the R&A with Densmore Shute and Craig Wood on the last green after the two-round playoff. Shute shot 75 and 74 to Wood's 78 and 76 to win.

Shute accepts the Claret Jug and thanks all concerned for helping to make it such a memorable tournament.

The presentation.

The new champion discusses past winners, whose names are engraved on the plinth, with two members of the Championship Committee.

Alan Dailey, an Englishman, played most of his shots with a cigarette hanging from his mouth! Representing Bradley Hall, he finished 11 shots behind the winner.

Leo Diegel and Craig Wood pose for George Cowie's camera at the side of the eighteenth green.

Jock Hutchison back on the links he was brought up on.

Walter Hagen opened up with a record-equalling 68 and led the field at the halfway point.

Left: Hagen's swashbuckling style attracted great crowds who stayed with him during his four rounds, despite finishing with two disappointing rounds of 79 and 82.

Andrew Kirkaldy gives Archie Compton some advice in his inimitable way. Andrew, or "Andra" as he was known, became a real character both on and off the course. Runner-up to Willie Park Jr in 1889 and to his brother, Hugh, in 1891, third in 1894, 1895, and 1899, he was prominent for many years for his forthright manner and quirky sense of humor.

Percy Alliss, father of Peter Alliss, was prominent in many Open Championships. He was third at the first Open in Carnoustie in 1931 and ninth the following year at Sandwich but, on this occasion, failed to make the last day's play.

Olin Dutra and Gene Sarazen seen here in relaxed mood, were both in contention up until the very last hole, just missing out on the play-off.

Left: Jack McLean, the leading Amateur, playing out of sand.

Ed Dudley (USA) driving, just three off the lead.

The 1934 Open Championship Medal for Sir Henry Cotton.

A sizeable scoreboard was installed at the Bow Butts behind the R&A. This ground was originally used for practising archery in the fifteenth and sixteenth centuries.

Henry Cotton sharpened up his game to good effect with rounds of 73, 71, and 72, but faded in the last round to lose by three shots. The next year the Englishman, representing Waterloo in Belgium, would win the first of his three Open Championships at Sandwich followed by Carnoustie in '37 and Muirfield in '48.

Syd Easterbrook, on the last green, just fails by one shot to join the play-off between Shute and Wood.

A threesome sitting comfortably against the starter's box, ready to play.

Paul Runyon hits cleanly out of a bunker on the second, but fails to make his mark in the tournament.

Pipe-smoking Archie Compton, despite this appendage when swinging, was a prodigious hitter of the ball. One of the fancied British players to do well, he played inconsistently over the four rounds but still managed to finish just four shots off the lead.

The whole of the American Ryder Cup team went up to the cathedral grounds to pay their respects to the Morrises, after the first day's play in the Open. Their captain, Walter Hagen, laid this wreath.

Above: During the Open Championship it was tradition that steam trains passing the sixteenth green would slow down and occasionally stop to let the competitors hole out!

Bobby Jones returned to St Andrews in 1936, unannounced, for a friendly four ball while staying at Gleneagles. When word got around, the whole town came down to greet him and follow him round the course. He had hardly played since his Grand Slam but, much to the delight of the admiring crowd, he reached the turn in 34. More and more people arrived on the course and by the time he came off the eighteenth green, mobbed by autograph hunters, you would have thought he had won yet another Open!

1939-1957

THE LEAN YEARS

THE RUN OF AMERICAN WINS IN THE OPEN SINCE 1921 STOPPED ABRUPTLY IN 1934.

DENSMORE SHUTE HAD RETURNED TO ST ANDREWS IN 1939 TO DEFEND HIS TITLE WITH

GENE SARAZEN, BUT THERE DIDN'T SEEM TO BE MANY OF THEIR COLLEAGUES ABOUT.

IN THE LEAD-UP TO THIS TOURNAMENT, HENRY COTTON HAD WON TWO, ALONG WITH

FELLOW COUNTRYMEN PERRY, PADGHAM, AND WHITCOMBE.

A group of Argentineans arrived for the first time and did well, with three out of four making the cut. One of them, Martin Pose, was actually in contention, until he grounded his club behind the 17th green in the third round. Not understanding his caddie or the rules official in their warnings that the grass in front of the wall was classed as a hazard, by grounding his club he incurred a two-shot penalty and scrambled for an eight. The Road Hole—in its usual unpredictable way—had claimed yet another victim.

Only Johnny Bulla from Chicago represented the USA in the last two rounds, after the field was cut severely to 34 competitors. He was close, finishing runner-up, just two shots behind the unexpected winner, Englishman Dick Burton.

Most of the spectators that week followed Henry Cotton and a young Bobby Locke around. South African Locke came in with a 70 in the first round despite an 8 at the 14th. The 5th and 14th had been lengthened, partly to ease crowd control problems. This move certainly made the 14th hole even more threatening than it had been, and Bobby Locke was the first to suffer on it. Hitting into one of "the Beardies" (a group of three bunkers) from the tee, he greedily left the ball in the bunker—going for distance—got out, and then carried into "Hell." He eventually holed a good putt for an eight. In the next round he tried to keep his drive away from the trouble down the left, but put his ball out-of-bounds on the right. Locke was two over par at the halfway stage, but five over for the fourteenth.

Dick Burton, by birdying the last, claimed the Claret Jug after battling bravely against a strong wind. He received a cheque for £100 for his scores of 70, 72, 77, and 71. The total prize money was £500.

It was unfortunate for him that shortly after he won the Open at St Andrews, war broke out and no product endorsements (not that there were many about) or exhibition matches were forthcoming. At least he could claim to be the longest reigning champion. It was over seven years before the competition started up again. For many years an English club professional at Coombe Hill just outside London, Burton played in three Ryder Cups and had the reputation of being the longest hitter of his day.

The crowd is eagerly awaiting the presentation to the Englishman, Dick Burton, who had broken the hold of the American dominance in St Andrews since 1921.

Left: Autograph hunting had become popular, especially with children, in the 1930s.

Below: There was great expectation when Henry Cotton arrived, having won in 1934 and again at Carnoustie in 1937, but it was not to be his Championship, finishing eight shots behind the winner.

"Waiting to play."

Sheltering from the rain during the morning of the third round.

Top, middle, and above: The first green, the fifteenth hole, and the seventeenth tee.

Sou'westers, Mackintoshes, and brollies were a necessity for spectators in the unpredictable weather that the Open threw up time and time again.

Reg Whitcombe, the defending champion, after his win at Sandwich in 1938 finished joint third, four shots adrift.

Five Argentinean golfers made the long trip over to play—three of them made the cut with Martin Pose finishing a respectable eighth, just five shots behind Burton.

Crowd control was still a problem, even on the first tee. Could a yappy dog be classed as a movable hazard?

Paul Runyon finds trouble in thick whin, which encroaches on the right-hand side of the fairway on most of the holes on the way out and around the loop. After checking his rulebook, he seeks help from a none-too-helpful-looking referee and, after much deliberation, "picks and drops" under penalty and plays on—but doesn't make the cut.

Old champions, Harry Vardon, six-time winner, having first won at Muirfield in 1896, accompanied by Ted Ray, who had also won there in 1912.

Bottom left: Two Englishmen, Dick Burton and Charlie Ward, stride down the fairway in a confident mood. Burton was four under and Ward one under after two rounds (the par still being 73 at that time). While Dick Burton marched on to glory, poor Charlie fell by the wayside with a last round of 83.

Below: Fighting a lone cause for America, Johnny Bulla, leading till the last round, just failed to win, and looks as if he were about to take a long walk out to sea after the result was announced.

As tension mounts in a typical east coast drizzle.

This caddie looks as if "his man" could not have broken 90 in the first qualifying round!

For green maintenance, long gone were the days of sheep grazing and scythes—from the first small hand-mower in 1882 to the larger horse-drawn grass cutters to this "state-of-the-art" mower from 1939. This one is being used to prepare the eighteenth green on the New Course for the qualifying rounds.

Archie Compton gets a lesson from this child on how to take the putter back in a straight line to the hole!

Cigar-smoking Billy Burke, from the USA, didn't make it through to the final day after the field was drastically cut to 34.

Dick Burton hits one high and long off the first tee in the final round.

Caddies eagerly show the line at the start of play. All the local caddies had nicknames such as, Sandshoe, Teacle Fenton, Trap Door, Skipper, Stumpie Eye, and The Barrel Dancer. The tall caddie on the left in this photograph is called "Hand me down the moon."

1946

WITH THE HELP OF GERMAN P.O.W.S THE OLD COURSE WAS KNOCKED BACK INTO SHAPE AND MADE READY FOR THE FIRST CHAMPIONSHIP SINCE THE WAR. IT SEEMED APPROPRIATE AFTER ALL THE TRAUMA AND UPHEAVAL OF THE LAST SEVEN YEARS THAT THE OPEN SHOULD START UP AGAIN WHERE IT LEFT OFF IN 1939, BACK AT THE HOME OF GOLF.

There was much talk of Byron Nelson coming over after his phenomenal run of victories on the American tour in 1945, but this did not materialise. Instead, the U.S. Open Champion, Lawson Little, arrived with Johnny Bulla, who was hoping to go one place better than last time. A reluctant Sam Snead followed, leaving just two days to familiarise himself with the course. He had played in the Carnoustie Open of 1937, but only because he was already over here as a member of the American Ryder Cup team.

Snead's first impression when arriving on the train, which cut right through the heart of the Linksland on its approach to the town, was "an old, abandoned kinda place, this." To add insult to injury, he was even less impressed with our big double greens, calling them "absurd"—in his defence he may have been tense or intimidated by them as his putting had gone downhill before he arrived.

Out of 268 entries, 100 qualified, and on the first day of the Championship proper, the long seven-year wait to defend his title must have gotten to Dick Burton, as he immediately sliced one out-of-bounds on the 1st tee. To his credit he steadied up and finished strongly with birdies at the 17th and 18th.

Norman von Nida, who led the qualifying, started well with a 70, as did the favourite, Henry Cotton, who matched his own score in the second round and led Sam Snead by a shot.

Dai Rees, the little Welshman, broke the long-standing record of Bobby Jones in 1927 with a 67 in the second round, much to the delight of the home crowd, who would from that moment on call him "The Welsh Wizard."

By day three Snead was justifying his nickname, "Slammin' Sam." He was the most prodigious striker of the ball, and through the week drove through the 9th, 10th, and 12th around the loop. Snead, Bulla, and Rees were tied going into the last round, with Cotton one behind. South African Bobby Locke had faded a bit after his opening 69 but was still dangerous.

Rees had an unsettling start under pressure from the expectancy of a volatile following. He silenced one of them when his opening drive hit him on the head and rebounded into play on the first. He then found the burn and took seven. Cotton, the other British hope, also found water at the start of his final round.

The wind had risen and made the first nine holes the hardest for a change, but Snead was unperturbed. He retained his balance and conviction, and won by four shots from Locke and Bulla. Poor Johnny Bulla—runner-up at St Andrews yet again.

Sam Snead won over 120 tour events and three Masters during his career. Despite his disparaging opening remarks about the Old Course and the town, locals all agreed that he was a worthy winner of the 1946 Open.

Sam Snead, on collecting the Claret Jug, declared that the Open was "just another tournament," though not at the presentation. He was also heard to say, "Whenever you leave the USA, boy, you're just camping out."

Sam Snead flirted with the "out-of-bounds" by the railing down the right of the opening hole on his last round in a difficult crosswind. He found two bunkers and a whin at the sixth, but managed to scramble for a six. As all his rivals fell away in blustery conditions, Snead got stronger and eventually cruised in with a four-shot cushion.

Henry Cotton and Mr Cyril Tolley, an amateur, representing the Royal and Ancient, in their first qualifying round on the New Course.

Roger Wethered, who had done so well in the 1921 Open, was Captain of the R&A in the year of the 1946 Open and escorted General Eisenhower around the Old Course.

Crowd scene at the sixteenth green.

Dai Rees created great excitement among the home support by breaking Jones's long-standing record by one shot with a 67 in the second round.

Below: Driving over the railway sheds on the seventeenth tee was a daunting prospect, especially if a train was on its way down the track. Unsighted, it would suddenly appear, more often than not, in the middle of a backswing!

An excited crowd greets the Championship Committee as they set up the table, ready for the presentation.

The walkie-talkie radio set was used for the first time on the course to relay information back to the scoreboard.

The scoreboard was the centre of attraction. As spectators milled around it, scores were relayed by portable radios for the first time at St Andrews.

Painting the new black and white flagpoles and freshening up and refurbishing the old tee boxes for the Championship.

View down the fifteenth with the lone exhibition tent in the distance.

Bobby Locke missing a short putt on the seventeenth. He then three-putted the last for a 76 to share second place with Johnny Bulla.

Sam Snead, in full control of his game, plays a long iron onto the fifth green.

Sam Snead holes out on the last green for an emphatic win in the first Open Championship since the war.

The first completed rounds start to be posted on the scoreboard.

BBC radio commentary had started with a portable booth which was moved around the course, arousing much interest from the spectators.

1955

THE OPEN TOURED EIGHT DIFFERENT VENUES BEFORE RETURNING TO ST ANDREWS. IT

HAD BEEN HOSTED BY HOYLAKE, MUIRFIELD, SANDWICH, TROON, PORTRUSH (IN

IRELAND), LYTHAM, CARNOUSTIE, AND BIRKDALE. DURING THIS PERIOD BOBBY LOCKE

WON THREE OF THEM, COTTON ANOTHER, WITH ONE AMERICAN WIN BY BEN HOGAN AT

CARNOUSTIE IN 1953, ON HIS ONLY CHAMPIONSHIP VISIT. IT WAS WORRISOME THAT

FRANK STRANAHAN, AT THAT TIME AN AMATEUR, WAS THE LONE AMERICAN VISITOR

SHOWING UP ON A REGULAR BASIS. HE WAS RUNNER-UP ON TWO OCCASIONS.

The fifties were dominated by Locke and Thomson. Australian Peter Thomson was the defending champion and was highly fancied to win it again.

Qualifying rounds were once more on the Old and New Courses. In 1895, when the New Course was described as "more hazardous than the Old," Hugh Kirkaldy had set the course record with an 85 on the day after the Open. Frank Jowle was 22 shots better in qualifying, the day before the Open, 60 years later!

George Fazio—who had lost in a play-off in the American Open in 1950—failed to make the cut, but U.S. Open champion Ed Furgol qualified comfortably, along with Byron Nelson, who had at last graced St Andrews with his presence.

Scotsman Eric Brown, "The Bomber," and "The Welsh Wizard," Dai Rees, opened their challenge with 69s. After two rounds the Scots were excited that maybe after all these years (since 1893) they'd have a home-based winner in Eric Brown as he set out in the third round tied for the lead with Peter Thomson. It wasn't to be. Thomson was quite solid in his play and resolute in his will to win. He fended off the challenge of Brown and the charge of Johnny Fallon, who had reduced the front nine to 31 shots on his way to a record-equalling 67.

Bernard Darwin, near the end of his journalistic career in reporting golf, said of Peter Thomson, "It is impossible to imagine a better temperament, marked by unruffled composure, courage and common sense."

That, and the wonderful balance and control he maintained consistently in his swing, won him the day. He broke the best Open aggregate at St Andrews—long held by Bobby Jones—by four shots, with scores of 71, 68, 70, and 72. He won £1,000—the first four-figure purse of the Open.

Thomson's record in the 1950s in the Open was astonishing, finishing 2nd, 2nd, 1st, 1st, 1st, 2nd, and 1st in 7 consecutive years. His few critics—who suggested he had an easy ride of it during this period—were silenced at Southport, England in 1965 when he won for the 5th time, with Nicklaus and Palmer trailing in his wake 9 and 10 shots adrift.

Those bunkers hidden from the twelfth tee were very much in view when the course was originally played in reverse.

Despite an adventurous seven at the fourteenth, Peter Thomson steadied up and with just the seventeenth hole to play, had a two-shot cushion over Johnny Fallon. He drove far and true on the Road Hole and secured his victory with a fine shot to the green.

Byron Nelson, playing at last in his first British Open, took a large gallery around the course with him, everyone knowing of his phenomenal run of tournament wins in the States. But on this occasion he finished 15 shots adrift. Paired with Henry Cotton and Fred Daly, who look more worried about the outcome of this drive than the player himself!

Bobby Locke bunkered.

Bobby Locke on the first tee was looking for his fourth win, having won in 1949 at Sandwich, Troon in '50, and Lytham in '52. Thomson had beaten him by a shot the previous year at Birkdale.

While waiting to start their round, Peter Thomson chats with Henry Cotton, past his prime but enjoying his golf, like Byron Nelson he finished 15 shots behind Thomson's record-breaking aggregate of 281, 11 under par.

Dai Rees driving at the first, fell back after his opening 69—ten shots worse off in the second round. He is watched by the future Centenary winner, Kel Nagle, and Ken Bousfield, who finished fifth that year.

Peter Thomson holes out for par and successfully defends his title.

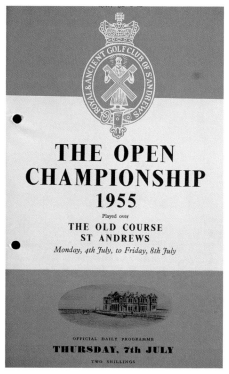

The BBC, on this occasion, gave its first live television transmission on the final day of the Open Championship and boosted the tournament's popularity. A decade later it would be truly international again thanks to the small screen.

The official programme cover of the 1955 Open.

A very young Gary Player played the Old Course that year—but not in the Open! He was soon to make his mark by coming in fourth at Hoylake in '56 and then winning at Muirfield in '59.

The reunion of past champions James Braid and Arthur Havers. James Braid had his last win of five Championships in 1910. Englishman Arthur Havers had stopped the defending champion, Walter Hagen, by a shot from winning again at Troon in 1923.

Peter Thomson is watched by Bruce Devlin as he plays a chip shot after dropping his ball, under penalty, from the burn at the first hole in a practise round—not a shot he would have to reproduce in the Championship proper.

The crowds surround the Road Hole on the last day of play.

1957

THE OPEN WAS BACK AFTER JUST ONE YEAR AWAY TO HOYLAKE, WHERE PETER THOMSON MADE THREE IN A ROW. WHO WOULD STOP HIM FROM EQUALLING YOUNG TOM'S RECORD OF FOUR CONSECUTIVE WINS? BOBBY LOCKE MIGHT, THOUGH AS ONE LOCAL CADDIE REMARKED, "HE'S LOOKIN' GIE PORTLY THAE DAYS!" OBSERVING THAT HE HAD PUT ON FOUR STONES (OR ABOUT 60 LBS) IN WEIGHT SINCE HE WAS RUNNER-UP TO SAM SNEAD IN 1946. TIPPED TO DO WELL WAS ANOTHER SOUTH AFRICAN, A YOUNG GARY PLAYER, WHO HAD BEEN FOURTH AT HOYLAKE.

Dr Cary Middlecoff, winner of The Masters in 1955, had just lost in a play-off defending his U.S. Open Championship, but he arrived fit and fresh. Although very methodical in his play (really slow), he attracted great attention during practice.

Locke posted his intention by leading the qualifying with Bernard Hunt, a fine English player, at 137. It was Eric Brown who grabbed the spotlight—as he had in 1955—much to the delight of the home crowd, with rounds of 67 and 72, two ahead of Locke. He was in the last match out, leading the field for the third day's play.

The Championship Committee had realised that with television covering the end of play for the first time, it would make more sense and create more excitement if all the main contenders were drawn against each other vying for position. Up until that point it was possible to win the Open by four hours as well as by four shots!

There was a five-shot swing back to Locke in round three after an inspirational 68, with Peter Thomson—his oldest and nearest rival—three behind. Both shot 70 in the final round and yet another Championship best aggregate was made at 279.

There was still drama to come—not because Locke had entertained the crowd with a song after the presentation (which he had)—but because there had been a complaint that he'd marked his ball incorrectly on the last green. When the Championship Committee met they decided that there had been no advantage gained, and that from four feet with a three-shot lead it would not have affected the outcome, and so the result stood.

The Old Course suited Bobby Locke's style of play, which was to draw the ball away from trouble and let it run. The large greens didn't inhibit him, for he had a deft putting touch. Locke enjoyed his visits to St Andrews, and every night without fail during the 1957 Open he could be heard singing "I Belong to Glasgow" after a few pints of beer in the St Andrews Golf Club. It obviously didn't affect his game or the outcome of that particular Open—club golfers take heart!

Locke had won four Opens, but the pressure of always being the centre of attention was taking its toll. He had travelled the world playing golf, but in 1959 he made Muirfield his last serious challenge, and fellow countryman Gary Player ably took over his mantle.

"Unlucky for some" but not for Bobby Locke, as he walks under a ladder propped against the Royal and Ancient Clubhouse, having just completed his first round in 69.

Below: The Scot, Eric Brown, leading at the halfway stage, is seen here playing off the 12th tee in the third round, but Bobby Locke pulled back five shots on him and Brown eventually finished third.

John Paton, another Scot in contention that year, is now the Honorary Professional to the R&A.

Advert from *Golf Monthly*.

Bobby Locke's controversial finish on the last green in the 1957 Open captured on camera.

Peter Thomson looking as if he has just won the Claret Jug. Bobby Locke had beaten him by three shots and broken his record aggregate for a St Andrews Open by two with a total of 278.

Below: Locke lines up his "wrongly-replaced" ball.

Grass so green, that had never been seen, before the '78 Open.

1960~2000

The Rebirth

of a

Championship

1960

THE CENTENARY OPEN IN 1960 WILL BE REMEMBERED FOR A RESURGENCE OF INTEREST AND STATUS FOR THE CHAMPIONSHIP. IT BECAME ONCE AGAIN THE MOST IMPORTANT MAJOR TO WIN. WAS IT THE CAVALIER ATTITUDE OF ARNOLD PALMER AT THE HEIGHT OF HIS CAREER THAT BROUGHT IT BACK INTO FOCUS INTERNATIONALLY, OR WAS IT THE PRESS AND TELEVISION COMING TO THE FORE?

It had been worrisome that from the 1933 Open—when six out of the top seven finishers were Americans—that the Americans' interest should dwindle. This was partly because "The Tour" became so established on the other side of the water. It seemed difficult to undertake such a long journey and expense for so little prize money. Exhibition matches had to be arranged throughout the country to supplement and justify the trip.

A persistent Gene Sarazen, who had won in 1932, kept returning to support the Championship. He constantly told his fellow professionals in the States that they hadn't achieved anything until they had won on a links course and in the British Open. It was hugely popular—and quite remarkable—that Sarazen should lead the qualifying in the Centenary Open on the New and Old Courses at the age of 58, nearly 30 years after his victory at Sandwich.

Arnold Palmer's high impact on the tournament with spectators and the press was no surprise, following his win at Cherry Hills in the U.S. Open with a typical Palmer charge in the last round. It seemed that the whole town and half the golfing population of Scotland had turned up to meet him. They weren't to be disappointed—Palmer did as he had to!

In an exciting last round Kel Nagle hung on. If only Palmer had holed his putts—which lipped and spun out on so many occasions—he could have strolled away with the Claret Jug. For the spectacle of it, the crowd was thankful he hadn't, as the Old Course yet again created high drama. Surely no other course in the world has such a sense of theatre about it.

After an eventful first two rounds—with Roberto de Vicenzo carding two record-breaking 67s and Nagle just two shots off the lead—Palmer must have wondered how on earth he'd make up a seven-shot difference. He'd have to watch his back, too, with Thomson one stroke and Player two strokes behind him.

After an eventful first two rounds, day three threw up a freak cloudburst near the end of the day's play. Nature itself had made a Palmer-like charge, and water poured down the hill from Martyr's Monument, cascading down the steps by the Royal and Ancient and quickly filling the Valley of Sin. The rain eased but did not stop all night, and play was suspended for what should have been the final day.

Thank goodness the committee had decided—partly through pressure from television—to stretch the Open over four days for the first time. In the past championships it had been tiring, both physically and mentally, to play the two qualifying rounds and the four regular rounds in three days. If that sounded like a hard grind, then think of Tom Morris versus Willie Park in the 1850s—a 36-hole challenge match? No—36 rounds! Twelve rounds at Musselburgh, twelve at North Berwick, and twelve at St Andrews—two rounds a day for three weeks, broken only by the two Sundays travel time to change venues!

A good drying breeze had unexpectedly put the course back in order for the final day's play. Palmer had clawed five shots back on de Vicenzo but only one on Nagle, who was now leading after day three. Playing in front of Nagle, Palmer must have frightened the life out of the Australian on the final day as he opened up with birdies on the 1st and 2nd holes and immediately reduced the deficit to two. Now it was to become a two-horse race. Nagle maintained his composure and, in fact, birdied the 7th and 8th. Both were out in 34 shots.

Palmer attacked every hole, but just could not get a putt to drop, while Nagle played steady par golf, protecting his four-shot lead. At last a birdie on the 13th got Arnie's army excited again. Nagle sputtered and had his first bogey on the 15th.

Palmer birdied the 17th after being in trouble over the road (the par for the Road Hole still being five at that time). Despite the tension there was banter between Palmer and Tip Anderson—a local caddie who was to become his life-long partner in Britain—as to what should have been done.

A 300-yard drive down the 18th, a flick onto the green, and a three-foot putt for a 68 left Palmer waiting to see if Kel Nagle's nerve would hold up on the 17th green. It did—a crucial 10-foot putt dropped. He eased the pressure on himself with a wonderful second shot on the last to two feet, and the Centenary Open was his. Palmer would get his revenge at Birkdale the following year, and yet again at Troon in 1962 with Nagle runner-up, six shots adrift.

The evergreen Gene Sarazen led the qualifying, much to the delight of everyone who followed him round.

Arnold Palmer, Frank Stranahan, and Gary Player stride down the first fairway in a practise round. Player was about to take a sharp turn to his left and return to Rusack's Hotel where he would change his trousers and return to the course, having been reprimanded by an official on the first tee for being "unsuitably attired!" Wearing one black trouser leg and the other white was Player's protest against apartheid.

Below: Palmer goes for the green at the tenth in the first round, in typical cavalier fashion, watched by an intense gallery.

Arnie crunches a three wood down the par-five fifth.

Below: If ever a swing could be classed as "poetry in motion," it must surely have been handed down from Allan Robertson in the 1840s to Harry Vardon in the 1890s and on to Bobby Jones in the '20s and Peter Thomson in the '50s—seen in the photograph at the finish of his swing.

The final scene at the Centenary Open.

Promoted as "The Great Challenge Match" like Morris vs Park 100 years earlier, Palmer and Player squared up to each other on one round of the Old Course in a televised "big money" match in 1961. Palmer won and pocketed $20,000.

"Ancient and Modern" —Willie Auchterlonie, winner of the Open at Prestwick in 1893 and Honorary Professional to the Royal & Ancient, introduces himself to the defending champion, Gary Player, during the Centenary celebrations on the eve of the championship.

Roberto de Vicenzo surrounded by spectators early on in the third round. After his sensational first two rounds of 67, he lost ground with a score of 75 as light rain turned to a downpour.

The steps by the Royal and Ancient turned into a waterfall as rainwater rushed down the hill, over blocked drains. It cascaded down the side of the 18th green into the Valley of Sin, which soon resembled a Loch!

The new champion looks pleased to be receiving a pair of Claret Jugs. The half-sized replica was made as a momento for the winner of the Centenary Open.

The cameraman perches precariously on the roof of an old Ford to gain a vantage point in recording the great event.

Kel Nagle, seated at the table, waits to be presented with the Claret Jug and the one-off
Centenary half-size replica. Everyone is just
about in place, but who is the young man
directly behind him? Is it the leading Amateur?
No, it is W.P. Robertson, the local electrician—
it's his microphone! As the supplier of this
equipment, he earned himself the right to stand
with Nagle and the dignitaries from the
Championship Committee for the presentation.
The electrician's father had worked the role in
the 1955 and 1957 Opens and took over the
duty again in 1964, managing to hog the lime-
light just as effectively! These were charmed
days indeed. Imagine such a family tradition
being maintained now!

There was something very final about the suspension of the third round of play! It left the crowd stunned, not to mention Arnold Palmer, who was making
his patented charge. A policeman was placed on duty to stop anyone from swimming up the last fairway!!

People milled around, long after the announcement was made that play was abandoned, still not quite believing what they'd seen.

The St Andrews fire brigade came to the rescue and seemed to enjoy their outing. They pumped water from the Valley of Sin, down the road running parallel to the eighteenth fairway and into the Swilken Burn.

Having withstood the enormous pressure of Palmer's final challenge, Nagle strode off the last green while offering a hand of commiseration to a disappointed but philosophical de Vicenzo. The popular Argentinian had ended up in a three-way tie for third place. Bernard Hunt, an Englishman, had caught up with a course record-breaking 66 and South African Harold Henning with a 69, to de Vicenzo's 73.

Local caddie "Tip" Anderson was ready to give advice on the line, as Arnold Palmer deliberates on how to hole yet another birdie opportunity.

The front cover of the official programme.

Part of the Centenary dinner table for the past champions, hosted by the Royal & Ancient (left to right) Arthur Havers 1923, Henry Cotton 1934, '37, and '46, Sir David Baird the past Captain, Willie Auchterlonie 1893, Sir Thomas Erskine, the Captain, and Gene Sarazen 1932.

1964

IT MAY HAVE LOOKED AS IF "CHAMPAGNE" TONY LEMA'S VICTORY—BY FIVE SHOTS—IN 1964 WAS EASY. HE WAS ALMOST CASUAL IN THE WAY HE WON AND THE WAY HE SAUNTERED AROUND THE COURSE IN WHAT SEEMED A HAPPY-GO-LUCKY MANNER. IT WAS HARDLY THAT, AS JACK NICKLAUS ROARED IN THE LAST ROUND, PULLING BACK EIGHT SHOTS, PLAYING A GOOD FEW MATCHES IN FRONT. LEMA STAGGERED TO THE 7TH TEE, TWO OVER, BUT A RUN OF FIVE CONSECUTIVE THREES MORE THAN STEADIED HIM. HE WAS SIX UNDER PAR FOR THE LAST TWELVE HOLES. FINISHING IN STYLE WITH A TRADITIONAL ST ANDREWS PITCH AND RUN THROUGH THE VALLEY OF SIN TO THREE FEET AT THE LAST, HE HOLED THE PUTT AND CLAIMED THE CHAMPIONSHIP.

After only one practise round he had played the course as he was told to—by Palmer's caddie, Tip Anderson—and generously said, as he handed out small bottles of champagne to the press, that it was 49% his win and 51% Tip Anderson's. But where was Arnold? Lema had just beaten him in a play-off for the Cleveland Open. Palmer had set his sights on the modern day's Grand Slam—the British and U.S. Opens, the Masters, and the PGA. Having finished fifth in the U.S. Open he felt tired and jaded, and much to everyone's disappointment he had decided not to come. But he suggested to Tony Lema that if he could get hold of Tip he should use him, for his local knowledge would be worth shots.

In the first round a strong wind turned to gale force in what Nicklaus described as the worst conditions he'd ever battled through. Even the refreshment tent, where many spectators took refuge, ripped and nearly blew away! Irishman Christy O'Connor's 71 in those conditions was heroic. Big

Jack hung on manfully to a 76. Peter Thomson could do no better than 79, along with the defending champion, Bob Charles, the one and only left-hander to win an Open. Player, Sanders, Henning, and Butler were just one shot better. Lema, walking off the last green after holing a 15-yarder, was more than content to have got the ball round in 73.

Having driven the 312-yard 12th and holed a 10-yarder for an eagle two, Lema waltzed in with a pair of 68s in rounds two and three. He looked unassailable until Nicklaus posted a record-breaking 66 and shot up the field, but it was too much ground to make up.

Lema now had his fifth win—the most important championship of the year—and it was still only July! That elegant flowing swing he had was the envy of many.

His "rags to riches" career was cut short dramatically in the summer of 1966 when he was killed in a plane crash on his way to yet another tournament venue. The golfing world had lost one of its most charismatic characters at the age of 32.

In late summer's early morning light, burnt grass turns golden.

A camera, being set up to record the presentation, aroused the interest of local spectators who had probably never seen one close-up before.

Part of the crowd broke ranks before the final approach shot was played.

Tony Lema arrived triumphantly to the safe haven of the last green as crowds swarmed around it, intent on being as close as possible to the final act of another memorable Open.

The adult seeking Jack Nicklaus's autograph is probably saying, in the time-honoured fashion, "It's not for me, it's for my boy!"

King Leopold (right) and his wife Princess de Rethy watch play, quite undisturbed...a far cry from the fuss made of Prince Leopold's visit during the week of the 1876 Open, which nearly ruined the town.

American short-game wizard Phil Rogers driving; lost in a play-off the previous year, had opening rounds of 74 and 79, and barely made the cut.

Fighting against strong crosswinds in the first round, Lema, under the watchful eye of his caddie "Tip" Anderson, plays a good recovery shot from the rough down the right-hand side of the third.

Escorted toward the recorder's hut, the new champion shows signs of the stress involved in achieving an Open win.

The one good spot to shoot a long shot of the 17th and 18th holes was from the old railway bridge. The line was closed in 1969 and the bridge dismantled shortly afterward.

Photographers take a break during a lull in play.

The admiring looks indicate that Michael Bonallack, five-times British Amateur Champion, has hit one down the middle of the first fairway. He did so again 35 years later in September 1999, playing himself into office as the new Captain of the Royal & Ancient.

No need for cardboard periscopes as an excited group of local children get a front-row view.

The Big Three, minus Palmer.

Irishman Christy O' Connor playing here to the sixth green drew a big crowd as he battled his way to a 68 in the last round and climbed the leaderboard to sixth place.

"Mixed fortunes" as Lema comes to the fore and Kel Nagle, the defending St Andrews winner, just makes the cut, but finishes last—34 shots behind.

The first full-color programme.

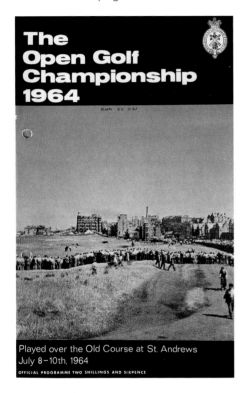

Despite a difficult uphill grassy lie at the thirteenth, Lema maintains his balance and control.

The Provost of St Andrews, T.T. Fordyce, wearing his chain of office, listened with pride as Tony Lema said emotionally that he was particularly pleased to have won this major championship in the home of golf.

1970

THE 1970 OPEN WILL ALWAYS BE REMEMBERED AS "THE MISSED PUTT AND THE PLAYOFF."

THE BRAVE BUT LUCKLESS DOUG SANDERS IN HIS COLOUR-COORDINATED ATTIRE,

AGAINST THE MIGHTY GOLDEN BEAR, JACK NICKLAUS.

Three qualifying courses had to be used, for at last there were exemptions for past champions and some of the top players. Palmer's no-show in 1964 must have influenced this.

There was great anticipation when Tony Jacklin stood on the 1st tee as current Open champion on both sides of the Atlantic. Even Britain's Prime Minister was there to see him off. The pressure on home-based Jacklin was enormous—but my goodness, what a start he made, birdying four of the first five holes. With another at the 7th, he laid up with his drive at the 9th, protecting his score, then holed a nine iron for an eagle two and an outward half of 29 shots. Jacklin did not buckle and was still aggressively threatening the hole on the way in when the heavens opened. It was uncanny—as if Tom Morris, watching from on high, had turned a hose on the champion to stop him from murdering his course! What had Jacklin done to deserve this? He cut a four wood on his second shot to the 14th into a whin in torrential rain, and as greens quickly flooded, play was suspended. After a sleepless night and an early start, Jacklin picked and dropped under penalty, and as a breeze came up he finished in 67 in what could or should have been one of the greatest rounds ever. Lee Trevino—who was to figure prominently in this Open—was to hand out two further body blows to Jacklin in the 1971 and 1972 Championships.

The Old Course was vulnerable as new standards in scoring were set. Twenty-five of the players who eventually made the cut were under 70 after the first round. The wind came up as Trevino led at the halfway stage with Nicklaus and Jacklin one behind. Neil Coles was well up the leader board after a record-breaking 65 in the first round, and Sanders, Horton, and Palmer were all within a shot.

A stiff wind on day three took care of and protected the reputation of the Old Course, with only two players breaking 70.

Trevino consolidated his lead, with Jacklin, Nicklaus, and now Sanders in second place. Fifty-seven players made the final day. Strong gusting winds made the flight of the ball unpredictable, and it was a hard slog for most to get to the turn. Only Nicklaus broke par on the front nine, and he was then the man to beat. Trevino's flair both to and on the greens seemed to desert him on the way in.

It was becoming a tense affair as Nicklaus bogied the 16th to give Sanders the lead for the first time. Nicklaus walked off the 18th thinking his chance had gone, but he could see the new leader in the dreaded Road Hole bunker. Anything could happen. What wasn't expected was that Sanders would get up and down quite comfortably from the bunker in two and then very uncomfortably play a poor pitch and three-putt the last.

As he stood frozen, so did the huge gallery. He addressed the "this to win the Open" three-footer, but stopped, and without moving his feet, bent down to flick away a piece of grass. He admitted later that he hadn't taken time to re-address the ball and pushed it sloppily by the hole. For two seconds there was an eerie silence broken suddenly by a collective gasp that swirled around the green like a mighty gust of wind, accompanied by a huge groan of disbelief.

A tie was declared and an 18-hole play-off (instead of the usual 36) saw Nicklaus and Sanders set off on Sunday in blustery conditions to settle the score. After 13 holes Nicklaus was four ahead but his worthy opponent came back at him and was within a shot by the 16th. Both holed out bravely for fours at the 17th.

After Sanders took the honour and drove just short of the green at the last, Nicklaus took off his sweater and—in one of the most cavalier shots ever hit in golf—belted one onto and through the green. Had he been slightly left of

the target, the ball would probably have bounded up the steps, past the R&A Clubhouse, continued bouncing up the hill to Martyr's Monument and disappeared on its way past the Cathedral, to splash into the harbour one mile away! Well, maybe not—but it was certainly one of the most ferocious and powerful blows ever witnessed. The banking of rough grass had stopped the ball, and he chipped back eight feet from the pin. Nicklaus holed the putt, and with a great release of tension and part elation, threw his putter into the air, almost braining Sanders as the club fell back to earth. Doug Sanders, with a shake of the hand, acknowledged that he was beaten, then for birdie holed a similar putt to the one he'd missed the day before.

Mark McCormack interviews Nicklaus and Sanders after a play-off is announced.

Nicklaus limbers up with Raymond Floyd about to walk onto the tee.

Two familiar sights are now gone from around the last green, The Golf Hotel, on the corner, (on the site where Allan Robertson had originally made his feather balls), and the whitewashed facade of The St Andrews Woollen Mill, next door to the Tom Morris Golf Shop.

With his hand firmly placed on the Claret Jug, Jack Nicklaus acknowledged what a titanic struggle it had been.

Willie Whitelaw, the great parliamentarian and Captain of the R&A that year, was ready to present the trophy, but would have to wait for the outcome of the next day's play-off to declare the winner.

Doug Sanders tentatively lays up three feet from the hole for the next infamous missed putt.

During the week Nicklaus attacked the hole on the last green, but, crucially, he also three-putted at the final hurdle.

Down the steps to the first tee and Sander's opening drive in the playoff.

Spectators watch for the next pairing to tackle and avoid disaster on the dreaded Road Hole.

Prime Minister Edward Heath wishes the current
British Amateur champion, Michael Bonallack,
well as the Championship gets underway.

The winning putt.

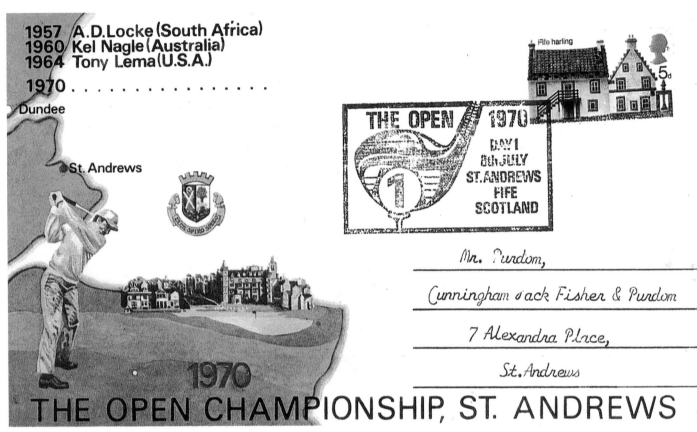

1957 A.D.Locke (South Africa)
1960 Kel Nagle (Australia)
1964 Tony Lema (U.S.A.)

1970 . . . .

Dundee

St. Andrews

1970
THE OPEN CHAMPIONSHIP, ST. ANDREWS

Fife harling

5d

THE OPEN 1970
DAY 1
8th JULY
ST.ANDREWS
FIFE
SCOTLAND

Mr. Purdom,

Cunningham Jack Fisher & Purdom

7 Alexandra Place,

St. Andrews

The first ever first-day cover to commemorate the Open!

The victor and the vanquished.

Sanders gets up and down in 2 from the Road Hole bunker—a par 4 at the last would win him the Open.

"The Power and the Glory"—Nicklaus crunches one down the second.

The Past Champions' Dinner—with 27 wins between them from 1923 to 1969. Left to right back row: Arthur Havers (1923), Gene Sarazen (1932), Dick Burton (1939), Fred Daly (1947), Roberto de Vicenzo (1968), Arnold Palmer (1961 and '62), Kel Nagle (1960), Bobby Locke (1949, '50, '52, and '57), Henry Cotton (1934, '37, and '48), and Peter Thomson (1954, '55, '56, '58, and '65). Front row: Densmore Shute (1933), Bob Charles (1963), Max Faulkner (1951), Jack Nicklaus (1960), Tony Jacklin (1969), and Gary Player (1959 and '68).

1978

THE CHAMPIONSHIP RETURNED TO ST ANDREWS AFTER BACK-TO-BACK WINS BY LEE

TREVINO AT BIRKDALE AND MUIRFIELD IN 1971 AND 1972. TOM WEISKOPF WON AT TROON

THE FOLLOWING YEAR, GARY PLAYER HAD HIS THIRD IN THREE DECADES AT LYTHAM,

TOM WATSON HAD HIS FIRST WIN AT CARNOUSTIE, JOHNNY MILLER WON AT BIRKDALE,

AND WATSON WON AGAIN AT THE NEW VENUE—TURNBERRY.

Watson and Jack Nicklaus were six-to-one joint favourites. Their epic head-to-head at Turnberry the year before left their nearest rivals 10 shots adrift.

When Arnold Palmer won by a barrowload at Troon in 1962, Nicklaus was 29 shots behind him on his first appearance. From then on it was to be a different story. Everyone knows of Nicklaus's unique achievements in tournament golf over so many competitive years. Braid dominated a period of the early 1900s, Hagen and Jones in the 1920s, Thomson and Locke in the 1950s, and Tom Watson in the early 1980s.

No one can match Nicklaus's consistency through his long and distinguished career in the Open. He was 3rd in 1963, then 2nd, 13th, 1st (at Muirfield in 1966), 2nd, 2nd, and 6th before winning at St Andrews in 1970—5th, 2nd, 4th, 3rd, 3rd, 2nd, and 2nd again, before defending and winning once more. During the early to mid 1970s he had won the Masters twice and the PGA three times, while picking up 26 victories on the American circuit.

Playing in a St Andrews Open Championship must surely be the longest week of any professional's life—desperately wanting to do well, psychologically up there on the leader board on the first tee at the start of day one. The halfway stage normally starts to sort out the men from the boys. It may sound unkind to say that there's occasionally "a flash in the pan" up there amongst the top names, but it's rare that they will absorb the pressure and last the pace.

The Open was now truly international and for the first time in its history the Japanese had made an impact. After two rounds Isao Aoki was leading on five under with his compatriots—Masashi Ozaki and Tsuneyuki (Tommy) Nakajima—three under. Just ahead of them on four under was Severiano Ballesteros from Spain and Bob Shearer from Australia. Then came the Americans Crenshaw, Weiskopf, and Kite, followed by Palmer and Moody, with Nicklaus four off the pace. In there fighting for Britain were Peter Oosterhuis and a young Nick Faldo.

At one point in the third round there was a five-way tie, as Tommy Nakajima spent the longest five minutes of his career on and around the 17th green. With a long putt for a speculative birdie to join the leaders at five under, his ball meandered off-line and, slowly, cruelly into the Road Hole bunker—on the 18th tee he stood one over and out of contention. The only consolation for him was that from that moment on, the Road Hole bunker would always be known as "Nakajima's."

As Jones had done in 1927, just over 50 years later Jack Nicklaus strode across the Swilken Bridge and down the last fairway to rapturous applause. After the final day's play had swung one way and then another, Nicklaus found himself with a two-shot cushion over fellow Americans Floyd, Crenshaw, and Kite, all in the clubhouse. Paired with the relatively unknown New Zealander, Simon Owen (who had been leading up until the 16th), Nicklaus holed out and claimed his third and, surprisingly, his last Open title.

Nicklaus drives off with Englishman Peter Oosterhuis, who was in contention in both the 1970 and '78 Opens at St Andrews.

Bird's-eye view of the walkway across the seventeenth.

Top: Nicklaus's final putt to make him a double winner at St Andrews.

Above: Harry Carpenter introduces live coverage commentary for the BBC.

Left: Oosterhuis and Watson at their finish of play.

The ingenuity of the press tent disrupted by a postal strike during the 1978 Open.

Nicklaus goes to the top of the leader board with one hole to play.

A subdued crowd awaits the outcome as the leading contenders come into view.

A young Seve and his brother take on Andy Bean and Graham Marsh in a practise round.

Backstage at the Open.

Prior to the presentation, Keith McKenzie instructs the corps of official press photographers on what they may or may not do when photographing the new champion.

The press tent—typewriters under canvas.

Ben Crenshaw birdies the eighteenth to share second place with Owen, Floyd, and Kite.

The Claret Jug held aloft yet again.

Defending champion Tom Watson, in celebrated company, holds the trophy. Jack Nicklaus, behind him, would claim it back four days later.

Ivor Robson, still starting off every contender in the Open Championship today, about to introduce a relaxed Ben Crenshaw and Lee Trevino.

Who played the shots? Nicklaus's caddie looks emotionally drained.

An anxious moment on the tee on the outward half of the final round.

Simon Owen, who had unexpectedly led until overshooting the sixteenth green, congratulates the champion.

A moment of contentment—"It doesn't get much better than this."

1984

BY 1984 THERE WAS MUCH TALK OF TOM WATSON AND HIS FIVE OPEN WINS. ONLY SEVE BALLESTEROS IN 1979 AND BILL ROGERS IN 1981 HAD BROKEN HIS RUN. COULD HE EQUAL VARDON'S RECORD, OR EVEN SURPASS IT? CONSIDERING THE AMOUNT OF TALENT ON THIS, BY NOW, FIERCELY COMPETITIVE CIRCUIT, IT HAD BEEN AN INCREDIBLE ACHIEVE-MENT IN MODERN-DAY TERMS TO HAVE GOTTEN THIS CLOSE.

It looked more than possible when he stormed into the lead after a 66 in the third round. Watson found himself in the familiar position of playing "last couple" with Ian Baker-Finch, both at 11 under par.

It was ominous that Watson had caught up. Bernhard Langer and Seve would be out in front of them leading the way, two shots behind at nine under.

The Australians Graham Marsh and Greg Norman had great last rounds of 67 but had been too far off the pace, as had the American pair of Fred Couples and Lanny Wadkins. Sam Torrance finished well for Scotland—a third round 66 had given local supporters something to cheer about. Another Scot, Sandy Lyle, came in with a last round of 67. But they had all been too far behind the four main contenders to worry them.

All attention was focussed on the two matches still out on the course. Baker-Finch had immediately faltered. With the cruellest of luck he hit a solid wedge to the flag on the 1st, which landed close, then spun back viciously into the burn. He never recovered, and had a nightmare of a round, but he finished 3, 4, 4, 3 to save face and break 80, plummeting down the leader board to share 8th place with four others.

Langer just could not get his putter working to take

advantage, and put pressure on the other two after some fine iron shots on the way out. And so it became yet another head-to-head for Watson.

Tom Watson went ahead at the 10th after Seve dropped a shot at the 11th and failed with a birdie putt of four feet at the 12th. It looked like the American's day, but an uncharacteristic drive at the same hole found a whin bush and forced a penalty drop.

Now it really was getting down to the wire. The Spaniard birdied 14—Watson did likewise at the 13th. Seve Ballesteros, although still young, was tough, and he was up for the short battle ahead. As a typical seaside breeze got up he donned a "lucky navy blue sweater"—the one worn when winning at Lytham and at the Masters the year before.

They both parred 15 and 16 and were level. The 17th hole, which had terrified players throughout its history, would yet again decide the outcome of a close encounter. Seve drove left, flirting with the rough—luckily off a good lie and with 200 yards to the pin. Pumped up with adrenaline flowing, he hit a majestic six iron onto the green, and with two putts put the pressure back on.

Watson hit the perfect spot on the right side of the fairway, skirting the out-of-bounds—just a bit too close for comfort—but he calmly lined up with a two iron for yet another "most important shot of his life." As he was about to hit the ball a roar went up, signalling that Seve was close to the pin on his final shot to the last green. Watson settled again but pushed the shot badly to the worst position he could imagine—in a bad lie over the road two feet from the wall. He did well to scuttle the ball up to the green, but it was asking too much to hole a swinging ten-yarder. His heart must have sunk as he witnessed in the distance Ballesteros's birdie putt drop and heard the delight of the crowd as the Spaniard saluted them with that unforgettable "Olé."

Last day cover, signed by the winner.

View of play in progress down the second as, in the background, another group putts out on the last green.

Lee Trevino and the future winning American Ryder Cup team captain, Ben Crenshaw, talk with Championship Secretary, Keith McKenzie. Crenshaw holed in one at the eighth on the last day.

At 1:46pm, the last two couples prepare to make their challenge.

The leaders wait to play. It would be Watson's last great chance to equal Vardon's record of six wins.

Watson against the wall at the seventeenth.

With Watson needing a 2 to tie, some spectators were already making their way back to their cars to try to beat the traffic!

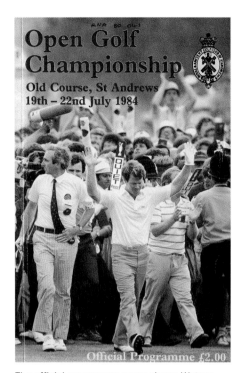

The official programme cover shows Watson, the defending champion, acknowledging the crowd after a bravely struck two iron to Birkdale's last green gave him his fifth win.

Lee Trevino, in his inimitable way, "fandangos" off the tee!

Michael Bonallack escorts the new champion and trophy down the last fairway.

The, by now, familiar lineup of past champions, with Watson yet again defending the Championship.

Ballesteros sets the ball off on its road to
glory...the rest is history!

1990

I THINK TOM MORRIS WOULD HAVE TURNED IN HIS GRAVE AT THE THOUGHT OF NICK

FALDO STANDING ON THE 1ST TEE ON THE FINAL DAY OF THE 1990 OPEN, 17 UNDER PAR.

OLD TOM WAS IMPRESSED ENOUGH WHEN J.H. TAYLOR, SANDY HERD, AND WILLIE FERNIE

WERE THE FIRST EVER TO BREAK 80 IN THE SECOND ROUND OF THE 1895 OPEN. J.H.

TAYLOR DID IT TWICE, AND WON BY FOUR SHOTS. HE BECAME ONE OF ONLY FOUR DOU-

BLE WINNERS HERE BY KEEPING ALL HIS ROUNDS UNDER 80 AND WINNING BY EIGHT

SHOTS IN 1900.

The first man to break 70 in an Open at St Andrews was Bobby Jones in his first round on the way to winning in 1927. Peter Thomson was the first to break par on every round when he held the trophy aloft in 1955. Ballesteros just failed—with a 70 in the third round—to keep all his scores in the 60s in the 1984 Open.

With a record score of 18 under par, Nick Faldo collected a cheque for hundreds of thousands of pounds. Jack Burns was left counting his £8 purse for winning in 1888. Although the total prize money nearly doubled from 1984 to 1990 to £825,000, the total prize money dropped dismally from £27 to £20 between 1885 and 1888.

The 1990 Open was to break all records, not just for Faldo's lowest winning aggregate, but for record crowds—over 200,000 spectators for the week; record lowest score of 63 from Paul Broadhurst; a record-equalling 132 by Greg Norman and Nick Faldo for the first two rounds (Henry Cotton had done it in 1934); Faldo shooting less than 200 for three rounds; and St Andrews now equalled Prestwick in hosting the most Open Championships.

The course itself was considered to be in its best condition ever, under the supervision of "The Keeper of the Green" Walter Woods. Some critics said that the Old Course was becoming incapable of defending itself!

Another alarming statistic was the lowest cut in an Open at one under. Arnold Palmer came in on level par, and although he received a hero's welcome it was slightly subdued, for spectators were saving themselves for the final day to show their real appreciation—but it was not to be. Sadly, Ballesteros and Watson, drawn together over the two days, weren't to make it either. Nicklaus was through, and would make the final day for the 28th time.

The third round on Saturday afternoon will be remembered as a confrontation between Faldo and Norman, both ten under as they set off to play together. The Australian came home nursing his wounds, nine shots behind Faldo, who had shot a flawless 67.

It really wasn't until the 58th hole—the 4th in the last round—after being bunkered on the left side of the green that Faldo felt he'd dropped a shot. He had played the 17th with respect, as a par-5, sensibly not taking any chances with the danger that lurked in "going for it."

On the last day, Baker-Finch was yet again in a final pairing at the Open, after a 64 in the third round. He would go on to win the next year, but from then on struggled to find his game.

The wind was quite strong, blowing from the east. The pin placements made scoring difficult, but Mark McNulty managed seven birdies and finished joint second with Payne Stewart five shots behind the winner. Faldo's seemingly unassailable lead was actually reduced to two shots by Stewart, but he drove into the "coffin" bunker at the 13th and his challenge fell away. His colourful attire made the rest of the field look like a company of accountants. One reporter said of Stewart's "Stars and Stripes" outfit that he looked as if he were ready to be buried at sea with full military honours!

As a young man, Nick Faldo quickly established himself on the circuit. He decided, when he was 28 years old, to rebuild his swing. Five years later he had won four majors. No one in Britain has, in recent times, made such an impact internationally—in the Masters, in the Ryder Cup, and in the Open itself. He put his win in St Andrews down to his iron play and his putting, holing out for 20 birdies and two eagles on his way to victory.

The worthy winner renews his acquaintance with the trophy and would again have it in his grasp for a third time at Muirfield in 1992.

Payne Stewart receives his runner-up cheque.

Baker-Finch and Faldo drive at the second.

Nick Faldo, in trouble for the first time in his four rounds, bunkered at the fourth.

Greg Norman hits sand.

Author David Joy, in his famous guise as Tom Morris, swaps hats with his friend, Lawrence Levy, who photographed many Opens up until his untimely death prior to the 1995 Championship.

Still practising after a 30-year partnership—"Tip" and Arnold Palmer.

Faldo burns up the course!

Fly past of the Red Arrows during the presentation.

The lineup for yet another past Champions' Dinner: Back row from left to right: Weiskopf, Ballesteros, Norman, Nicklaus, Faldo, Jacklin, Charles, and Lyle. Front row from left to right: Trevino, Watson, Palmer, Daly, Thomson, and Player

Greg Norman, having laid up to the left of "The Principal's Nose," plays to the sixteenth green.

The confrontation between Faldo and Norman, in the third round, left the Australian nine shots adrift.

Nick Faldo eagles the last in spectacular fashion on his opening round.

Opposite top: An early morning mist hangs low over the Old Course. Television cameras are covered and stands lie empty. Silence is broken as greens are hand-mown and new pin positions cut in preparation for day two.

Opposite bottom: Long shadows enhance the drama of the traditional stampede down the eighteenth fairway.

Not since Vardon in 1914 has a British player had such a high profile in the world of tournament golf.

From the roof of the St Andrews Golf Club the scene is set as Faldo, surrounded, marks his ball as Baker-Finch clears the stage for the Englishman's resounding victory.

1995

THE YEAR 1995 WAS THE 25TH ANNIVERSARY OF OPENS HOSTED AT ST ANDREWS. THERE

WERE 159 COMPETITORS TAKING PART, WITH ONE-THIRD OF THE FIELD BEING

AMERICAN. ON THE FIRST DAY'S PLAY THE WIND GOT UP EARLY AND HUNG ABOUT UNTIL

THE RESULT WAS ANNOUNCED. THE WIND WAS SOMETIMES BLUSTERY, SOMETIMES VERY

TRYING, AND SOMETIMES JUST IRRITATING! THE OLD COURSE MADE THE MOST OF ANY-

THING THAT BLEW—IT IS PART OF ITS CHARACTER IN THE WAY THE COURSE IS SHAPED.

IT BLOWS ACROSS YOU LEFT-TO-RIGHT, PULLING AT YOU AROUND THE LOOP, AND ON

TURNING ROUND AT THE 12TH, BLOWING YOU RIGHT-TO-LEFT. THE ONLY RESPITE IN

SUCH CONDITIONS IS TO BE PLAYING DOWNWIND AT THE 18TH.

Tom Watson was used to Links play by now, and he opened with a round of 67, finishing strongly, with 31 on the back nine. Ben Crenshaw, John Daly, and Mark McNulty matched his score. Nicklaus was in hell when he took 10 at the 14th (Hell bunker was the cause). He finished 78 but rallied with a 70 on a painfully slow second day's play and just made the cut—along with eight others—thanks to the leader, John Daly, three-putting the last.

Constantino Rocca was sharing second place with Daly, Brad Faxon was six under, Ernie Els was one shot ahead of Pavin, Cook, and Crenshaw, and another two Americans, Leonard and Stewart, were also in contention. Nick Faldo, with a 67 in the second round, had stepped up a gear, and the big (six-foot, eight-inch) Scottish amateur, Gordon Sherry, was on the leader board at three under.

Near the end of day two was Arnold Palmer's farewell to the Open Championship. Aged 65, he paused but didn't linger on the Swilken Bridge while he waved goodbye to rapturous applause. In the press tent shortly afterward he opened his interview by saying, "I guess it's all over." That will never be, for as his game fades, the impact made by Palmer, the man, will always shine through.

On day three Michael Campbell, a New Zealander, charged through the field to nine under, leaving Rocca and Daly—still playing around the turn—a lot to do. Crenshaw uncharacteristically three-putted the 9th and 10th and faded from the picture, much to everyone's disappointment. Ben's love of the traditions and heritage of the game are well known, and for him to win at St Andrews would have been fitting. That persistently nagging wind had Stewart, Faxton, Pavin, and Tomori all digging in. Steve Elkington came to the fore with his second 69 of the tournament.

In the last round it was like shuffling a pack of cards as players made their move to the front, then back again. Campbell could not master the conditions this time round. Sam Torrance, the Scot, had a look through the door early on, then it closed on him. Brooks—a 34-year-old Texan who broke the course record at Ladybank in qualifying—had been there or thereabouts and was within two shots until a six at the 16th put an end to his chance. Where was Tiger Woods while this was all going on? He was back in the clubhouse seven over par. "Steven who?" was the reaction when Steven Bottomley, an English pro, came to the fore and had his best week ever, with the only score under 70 by anyone remotely in contention on the last day. Steve Elkington played the most solid golf, but could not sink the crucial putts needed to worry those in front of him.

Yet another great climax to the Open Championship had begun when John Daly—whose touch around the greens was even more impressive than his immense power—faltered at the 16th. He'd had his luck at the 9th after a wild drive down the left that should have finished embedded in a whin found a path instead and an escape route to the green.

At the 17th, still in the lead, Daly found the face of the Road Hole bunker. He managed to blast out (probably increasing its depth by two feet!) but dropped a shot. Playing behind him, Rocca found the other main hazard on this hole—the road. He was forced to putt out of a rut.

The ball jumped out, and with a friendly kick up the grassy slope, stopped four feet from the flag. He then holed out for par.

On the last hole he drove well up the fairway, slightly left, and needed a deft but positive chip and a putt to win. He stubbed it! The ball ran almost apologetically 15 yards into the Valley of Sin.

As Daly was thinking about his acceptance speech, Rocca struck his putt on its "Mission Impossible." Up the steep slope it sped. It soldiered on another 40 feet until it spotted the hole, made a last mad dash for it, and dived in! The roar that went up as Rocca sunk to his knees must have been heard in Carnoustie.

A play-off of four holes followed immediately, with neither man having much time to compose himself. Rocca three-putted the first. Daly was resolute in holing a 30-footer for birdie at the 2nd and gave himself a welcome two-shot cushion turning round to play the most dangerous hole on the course. With three to get out of the Road Hole bunker, Rocca accepted defeat.

At 10:00 the next morning, when the wind and crowds had gone away, John Daly stood on the Swilken Bridge with the Claret Jug glinting in the sun having his photograph taken. A few passersby tentatively approached and like in a dream had their picture taken with the new Open Champion and the trophy—the same trophy that had first been held aloft in St Andrews by Tom Kidd 123 years before.

The Last Farewell.

The presentation—John Daly thanks everyone involved.

Michael Campbell nearly holes out from the Road Hole bunker in an inspired third round.

"Kindred spirits"—Daly and Rocca despite differences in lifestyle and nationality, have a common bond—a sharing of this great game, no matter how fiercely competitive it may become at times.

Near the finish of a practise round, an intrigued Gary Player is shown where a hidden camera had been installed in the Road Hole bunker to enhance the drama surrounding anyone caught by it.

John Daly at the top of his familiar extended backswing attracted big crowds with his cavalier style of play and surprised many with his deft touch in mastering the Links.

Tiger Woods failed to stamp his authority on the Old Course, despite all the hype surrounding him, and finished seven over.

A young lady rushed onto the course and presented Nick Faldo with a flower as he made his way down the first fairway. The gesture bowled him over!

A world-famous traditional view with a man well aware of its significance—Ben Crenshaw—aiming down the line of the clock on the Royal and Ancient Clubhouse.

Three past champions out on the course—Faldo, Norman, and Nicklaus.

No one expected this to go in, least of all Rocca, as the final moments took yet another dramatic twist.

Opposite page: Constantino Rocca fluffs his wedge into the Valley of Sin and thinks his chance to win has gone.

The foundation laid for the new sixteenth championship tee.

The laying of the turf on the new fifteenth tee.

The reconstruction of "Hell!"

The manicuring of the Road Hole bunker. After refacing and reducing its width, it looks even more demanding than before.

WHEN THE CROWDS ARE LONG GONE AND THE STANDS DISMANTLED, AN EERIE STILL-
NESS LINGERS AS THE COURSE RESTS AT THE SETTING OF THE SUN. SHADOWS OF THE
PAST CREEP ON TO THE COURSE AND SOUNDS OF DISTANT VOICES HERALDING TRIUMPH
OR DISASTER SEEM TO ECHO AROUND THIS HALLOWED GROUND WHICH IS THE OLD
COURSE, IN ST ANDREWS—THE HOME OF GOLF.

Masakuni Akiyama
220 (top), 220 (bottom), 222

AP/Wide World Photo
227, 228

British Golf Museum-St Andrews
125 (top right), 125 (bottom right)

Michael Brown
99 (bottom), 105

Corbis/Bettmann-UPI
174 (bottom), 185 (top right)

The Cowie Collection/St Andrews University Library
17 (top right), 40 (left), 47 (top), 102 (bottom right), 121, 124 (middle), 128 (top left), 128 (bottom left), 128 (top right), 128 (bottom right), 129 (top left), 129 (middle left), 129 (bottom left), 129 (top right), 130 (top left), 130 (middle left), 130 (bottom left), 130 (top right), 130 (bottom right), 131 (top left), 131 (middle left), 131 (bottom left), 131 (bottom right), 132 (top left), 132 (bottom left), 132 (top right), 132 (bottom right), 133 (top), 133 (bottom), 137 (top), 137 (bottom left), 137 (bottom right), 138 (top left), 138 (bottom left), 138 (top right), 138 (middle right), 138 (bottom right), 139 (top left), 139 (bottom left), 139 (top right), 139 (bottom right), 140 (top left), 140 (bottom left), 140 (top right),
140 (bottom right), 141 (top), 141 (middle left), 141 (bottom right), 142 (top left), 142 (bottom left), 142 (top right), 142 (bottom right), 143 (top left), 143 (bottom left), 145, 146 (top left), 146 (bottom left), 146 (top right), 146 (bottom right), 147 (top), 147 (bottom), 148 (top), 148 (bottom right), 149 (top), 149 (bottom), 150 (bottom left), 154 (top), 154 (bottom), 155 (upper left), 155 (middle left), 155 (bottom left), 155 (upper right), 155 (bottom right), 156 (top left), 156 (bottom left), 157 (top), 157 (bottom), 159 (top), 159 (bottom), 160 (top left), 165, 166 (top), 166 (bottom), 167 (top), 167 (bottom), 168 (top), 168 (bottom), 169, 170 (top), 170 (bottom), 171 (top), 171 (bottom), 178 (top), 178 (bottom), 179 (top), 179 (bottom), 180 (top), 180 (bottom), 181 (top), 181 (bottom), 182 (top), 182 (bottom), 183 (top), 183 (bottom), 184 (top left), 184 (top right), 187, 188 (top), 188 (bottom), 189 (top), 189 (bottom), 190 (bottom left), 190 (top right), 190 (bottom right), 191 (top), 191 (bottom), 192 (top), 192 (bottom), 197 (top), 197 (bottom), 198 (top), 198 (bottom left), 198 (bottom right), 199 (top), 199 (bottom), 200 (top), 200 (middle), 200 (bottom), 201 (top), 201 (bottom), 202 (top), 202 (bottom)

Golf Illustrated
40 (right), 79 (top left), 107 (top left), 107 (bottom left), 107 (top right), 107 (bottom right)

Golf Magazine
88 (right)

Golf Monthly
160 (top right)

David Joy
30 (top right), 31 (top right), 34 (top left), 82 (top)

Ian Joy Photographic
25 (bottom left), 25 (bottom right), 172 (top), 195, 203 (top), 203 (bottom), 207 (bottom), 208 (bottom left), 208 (top right), 208 (bottom right), 209 (bottom), 215 (top), 215 (bottom), 216 (top left), 216 (bottom left), 216 (top right), 216 (bottom right), 217 (top left)

Lawrence Levy
210 (right)

Iain Macfarlane Lowe
1, 4, 6, 8, 11, 13 (top left), 13 (bottom), 18 (top right), 19 (top), 19 (bottom), 20, 21, 23, 24 (top right), 28 (top left), 28 (bottom left), 31 (middle left), 33, 34 (bottom middle), 35 (left), 35 (middle left), 35 (middle right), 35 (right), 42 (top left), 45, 48, 49, 51, 54, 55, 56 (top), 56 (bottom), 57, 58, 60, 61, 62 (top), 62 (bottom), 63, 64, 65 (bottom), 66, 67, 68 (top), 68 (bottom), 69, 70, 72, 74, 75, 77 (top), 77 (bottom), 81, 83 (top left), 83 (top right), 85, 88 (top left), 90, 103, 106 (top left), 106 (top right), 106 (middle right), 106 (bottom right), 109 (bottom left), 113 (top left), 113 (top middle), 113 (top right), 113 (bottom right), 114, 118 (bottom), 123, 124 (right), 127, 131 (top right), 134, 148 (bottom left), 151 (bottom), 153, 156 (top right), 162, 177, 185 (top left), 185 (bottom), 210 (left), 229 (bottom), 230 (bottom), 231 (top left), 231 (top right), 231 (bottom), 234, 235, 236, 237, 239

The Sidney L. Matthew Collection
122

Fred McKenzie
39

Brian D. Morgan
223, 225

Prestwick Golf Club
24 (bottom left), 25 (top left), 25 (top right), 27 (left), 27 (right), 78 (bottom)

Royal & Ancient Golf Club
26 (top right), 41 (bottom left), 41 (top right), 108 (bottom)

St Andrews Preservation Trust
34 (top right), 46 (left), 46 (right), 83 (bottom), 88 (middle left), 88 (bottom left), 108 (top), 119 (top)

St Andrews University Library
14 (top), 24 (bottom right), 98 (bottom)

Phil Sheldon
194 (left), 205 (left), 205 (right), 209 (top), 211 (top), 211 (bottom), 212 (left), 212 (right), 213 (left), 213 (right), 217 (bottom), 218 (top), 218 (bottom), 219 (top), 219 (bottom), 221, 226 (top), 226 (bottom), 229 (top), 230 (top), 232, 233 (top), 233 (bottom)

Norman Spittal
193 (top), 207 (top)

Tait Family
94, 97 (top right)

D.C. Thompson & Co. Ltd.
117, 118 (top left), 118 (top right), 125 (bottom left), 143 (top right), 150 (top), 150 (bottom right), 151 (top), 156 (bottom right), 161 (top), 161 (bottom), 172 (bottom), 173 (top), 173 (bottom), 174 (top), 175 (bottom), 184 (bottom), 193 (bottom), 194 (right), 204 (top), 204 (bottom)

The Valentine Collection/St Andrews University Library
97 (bottom)

Vanity Fair
79 (top right), 89 (top left), 89 (top right)

G.W. Wilson Collection/Aberdeen University Library
96 (top)